MW01044786

GREEN BAY PACKERS

YESTERDAY & TODAY ™

CHUCK CARLSON
FOREWORD BY JERRY KRAMER

WEST
SIDE
PUBLISHING

Chuck Carlson has been a sportswriter and columnist for more than 30 years at newspapers across the United States. For 11 seasons, he covered the Green Bay Packers for the *Post-Crescent* in Appleton, Wisconsin. Carlson has written several books about the Packers, including *Titletown Again; The Green Bay Packers Pocket Primer; Tales from the Packers Sideline;* and *Brett Favre: America's Quarterback.* Carlson and his family currently reside in Wyoming.

Jerry Kramer played for the Green Bay Packers from 1958 to 1968 and was an integral part of the famous "Packers Sweep." Kramer has coauthored four highly acclaimed books, including a volume on his coach entitled *Lombardi: Winning Is the Only Thing. Inside the Locker Room,* Kramer's secret recordings of Vince Lombardi's locker room talks, is available on CD at www.jerrykramer.com.

Additional Consulting: Marty Strasen

Factual verification by Nathan Rush and Kathryn L. Holcomb

Special thanks to the City of Green Bay, Mary Jane Stodola, collectors Matt Erlandson and Jim Zimmermann; Mark Schneider of Glory Days Sports Pub; Mike Worachek at Packer City Antiques; Jeanine Meade and the Neville Museum; all the friendly folks at Titletown Brewing Company; and the helpful people at the Packers Hall of Fame, especially Aaron Popkey and archivist Tom Murphy.

Front cover photos (left to right): Curly Lambeau, Bart Starr, the "Ice Bowl," Vince Lombardi, Aaron Rodgers

Back cover photos (left to right): Paul Hornung, Reggie White, Don Hutson, Ray Nitschke

Yesterday & Today is a trademark of Publications International, Ltd.

West Side Publishing is a division of Publications International, Ltd.

Copyright © 2009, 2011 Publications International, Ltd. All rights reserved. This book may not be reproduced or quoted in whole or in part by any means whatsoever without written permission from:

Louis Weber, CEO
Publications International, Ltd.
7373 North Cicero Avenue
Lincolnwood, Illinois 60712

Permission is never granted for commercial purposes.

ISBN-13: 978-1-4127-6116-1
ISBN-10: 1-4127-6116-6

Manufactured in China.

8 7 6 5 4 3 2 1

Library of Congress Control Number: 2009923894

Front cover: **AP Images** (top left & top center); **Corbis** Larry Smith/epa (top right); **Getty Images** (bottom left); **Diamond Images** (bottom right)

Back cover: **AP Images** (right center); **Getty Images** (left center); **NFL** (left & right)

AP Images: 11 (left), 27 (right), 32 (top right), 34 (top), 35 (top), 39 (left), 43 (top right), 55 (left), 62 (left), 66 (top), 67 (bottom), 72 (bottom), 75 (top left & top right), 82 (bottom), 83, 97, 99, 105 (left), 106, 111, 112 (right), 118 (left), 119, 123 (bottom), 125 (left), 129, 135 (left), 138 (top), 142 (bottom), 146 (top); **City of Green Bay:** 154 (top left center); **Corbis:** Bettmann, 24–25, 82 (top), 90 (right); Lewis DeLuca/*Dallas Morning News,* 153 (bottom); Greg Fiume/NewSport, 137 (right); Allen Fredrickson/Reuters, 136 (left), 150 (bottom); Matt Freed/Zuma Press, 153 (top); John Gress/Reuters, 142 (top); G. J. McCarthy/*Dallas Morning News,* 152; Tannen Maury/epa, 158; Underwood & Underwood, 16 (bottom); **Ed Monette Collection:** 80 (top right); **Getty Images:** contents, endsheets, 6 (left), 32 (bottom right), 58 (bottom), 59 (left), 71 (top), 74 (left & bottom right), 93 (top), 96, 103 (left & bottom right), 108 (bottom), 109, 110, 112 (left), 116–117, 118 (right), 121 (right), 122 (left), 123 (top), 124, 126 (left), 127, 128 (bottom), 129 (left), 132 (left), 134 (left), 138 (bottom), 139, 140 (right), 141 (right), 143 (left & right), 144 (top), 145 (top right), 146 (bottom), 147, 150 (top), 151 (bottom); AFP, 140 (top); *Sports Illustrated,* 58 (left), 66 (bottom); **Green Bay Packers Organization:** 144 (bottom); **Courtesy Green Bay Packers Hall of Fame:** 20 (top right), 24, 26 (left & top right), 28 (bottom), 30 (bottom left & bottom right), 31 (top right & bottom center), 40 (top left), 41, 42 (bottom right), 43 (bottom right), 47 (top right), 51 (right), 67 (top right), 69 (top right), 76 (top left), 77 (bottom center & bottom right), 80 (bottom right), 81 (top center, bottom center & bottom right), 84 (top left & right), 85 (bottom right), 94 (bottom right), 95 (top center & bottom left), 101 (top left), 102 (top), 114 (bottom right), 115 (bottom center), 122 (right), 148 (center & right), 154 (bottom left); **Green Bay Packers Hall of Fame Archive:** 8–9, 10, 18 (left, left center, right & right center), 22 (top right), 23 (bottom right), 28 (bottom), 33 (top), 35 (bottom left), 38 (left center), 40 (top center & bottom right), 42 (top right & bottom left), 43 (top left), 44, 47 (left), 53 (left center, center, right & right center), 54, 55 (top & bottom right), 60 (top center, top right & bottom), 61 (top center), 68 (bottom left & bottom left center), 71 (top right, bottom left & bottom right), 81 (top center), 84 (top center), 92 (right), 93 (bottom right), 95 (top left & bottom right), 100 (top left), 101 (top right & bottom right), 103 (top), 107 (left), 113 (left), 114 (top center, top right & bottom left), 115 (bottom left & bottom right), 154 (top center); **Jim Zimmermann Collection:** 108 (top), 130 (bottom left), 131 (top left & top center), 132 (right); **Matt Erlandson Collection:** contents, 17 (left), 37 (bottom left), 40 (top right), 46, 52 (right & center), 56 (right), 58 (top), 63 (right), 64 (top right), 68 (top left & top right), 74 (top), 77 (bottom left), 84 (bottom left), 85 (bottom left), 93 (bottom left), 107 (right), 145 (top left & bottom left); **MGB Collection:** 35 (bottom right), 37 (bottom right), 38 (right center); **NFL:** contents, 3, 6 (right), 7, 12 (left), 34 (bottom), 37 (top), 39 (right), 48–49, 51 (left), 53 (center), 62 (right), 64 (bottom), 65, 70, 72 (top), 75 (bottom left), 78 (left & bottom right), 79, 82 (left), 86–87, 88 (left & right), 89 (left), 90 (left), 91 (top), 92 (left), 98, 102 (bottom), 104 (top right), 105 (right), 113 (right), 120, 121 (left), 126 (right), 128 (top), 133, 134 (right), 137 (left), 141 (left); **Neville Public Museum of Brown County:** Courtesy Henry Lefebvre Collection, 50 (top); Courtesy Otto Stiller Collection, 13, 14, 15, 16 (top), 20 (top left & bottom right), 21 (top left, top right & bottom left), 22 (bottom left & bottom right), 23 (bottom left), 26 (bottom right), 45; **Packer City Antiques:** contents, 8, 18 (center), 19 (top), 20 (bottom left), 22 (top left), 23 (top, top left & top right), 28 (bottom), 29 (bottom), 30 (top left & top right), 31 (top left, bottom left & bottom right), 40 (bottom left), 42 (top left), 48, 56 (top), 57 (bottom), 61 (bottom left), 68 (bottom center), 69 (center, bottom left & bottom right), 73 (right), 76 (top right), 77 (top left, top right, left center & bottom left), 78 (top right), 80 (top left, top left center, top right center & bottom left), 81 (top right center & top right), 84 (top right center & left center), 85 (top left & bottom left center), 86, 88 (top), 89 (right), 91 (bottom), 94 (bottom left), 95 (top right & bottom center), 100 (top right, bottom left & bottom right), 104 (top left & bottom), 114 (top left), 115 (top left, top right & center), 116, 127, 130 (top center & bottom center), 131 (bottom right), 135 (right), 136 (right), 140 (bottom left), 145 (bottom right), 149 (top center & bottom center), 154 (top left); **PIL Collection:** contents, 12 (right), 17 (right), 19 (bottom), 27 (left), 29 (top), 33 (bottom), 36, 38 (right), 43 (bottom left), 46, 52 (left), 56 (top), 60 (top left), 61 (top left, top right & bottom right), 63 (center), 64 (top left), 67 (top left), 68 (bottom right), 69 (top left), 76 (bottom left, top center & bottom right), 81 (top left), 85 (top center, top right & bottom right center), 94 (top left & top right), 101 (bottom left & top right), 125 (right), 130 (top left, top right & bottom right), 131 (top right & bottom left), 145 (top center), 148 (left & bottom left), 149 (top left & top right, bottom left & bottom right), 154 (top right), 155, 157; Merv Corning, 11 (right); **© Sport Gallery Inc.:** contents, 32 (left), 59 (right), 73 (left), 75 (bottom right); **Wisconsin Historical Society:** 57 (top)

Additional photography: John Fix

Vince Lombardi (center) was a devout Catholic who studied the priesthood for two years as a young man. He chose a different career path instead, but he never wavered in his faith. Here, he leads his Green Bay Packers in a pregame prayer in the mid-1960s.

CONTENTS

Don Hutson & Curly Lambeau

A 1950s-era Packers doll

Paul Hornung

CHAPTER FOUR
THE LEAN YEARS

Assorted 1960s-era bottle caps

CHAPTER FIVE
RETURN TO TITLETOWN

CHAPTER SIX

Vince Lombardi

A Packers pin from the 1950s

Brett Favre

FOREWORD

By Jerry Kramer

I've been part of the Green Bay Packers organization for more than five decades now, and if there's one thing that I've learned during that time, it's that once you're a Green Bay Packer, you're always a Green Bay Packer. There's a connection to Packers fans that time and distance cannot break. Players come and go, but the fans remain a constant—a vital and crucial part of the Packers and their legacy. They are always cheering, celebrating, and supporting their team. No fans in the NFL appreciate what they have more than Packers fans. They know what it means for a city the size of Green Bay to still have an NFL franchise, and they guard it with a jealous pride.

In 1958, when Ray "Scooter" McLean selected me as Green Bay's fourth-round draft pick, who did the Packers choose ahead of me? Some linebacker from the University of Illinois named Ray Nitschke. And before that? An LSU fullback named Jim Taylor. The Packers' No. 1 pick that year was a tall, handsome All-American linebacker named Dan Currie. Although none of us knew it at the time, this was the draft that many people point to as the turning point for the franchise, which had struggled through the 1950s.

Jerry Kramer has coauthored four books: Instant Replay, Farewell to Football, Lombardi: Winning Is the Only Thing, *and* Distant Replay. *He also released* Inside the Locker Room, *a CD set with Vince Lombardi's locker room speech from Super Bowl II.*

We joined a Packers organization that already had many future All-Pros and Hall of Famers, such as Paul Hornung, Bart Starr, Ron Kramer, Forrest Gregg, Bob Skoronski, and Jim Ringo. Teammate Dave "Hawg" Hanner called it the most talented team he had ever seen.

But talent wasn't enough, and that first season we went 1–10–1, the worst record in franchise history. It got so bad that when we'd go out in the community, fans (and yes, they were just as loyal and as vocal then as they are now) were all over us, asking, "What's wrong with you guys?"

Eventually, we started unwinding after games in the cramped and sweaty stadium locker room, where we'd turn on the jukebox, have a few drinks, and try not to think about what had happened on the field.

But a big change was coming, and the real turning point for the franchise arrived from the New York Giants in the form of Vincent Thomas Lombardi. Lombardi had never been a head coach in the NFL before, and we knew very little about him except that as an offensive coordinator, he had complete control of a prolific Giants offense. He started making changes the moment he arrived, and nothing in Green Bay would ever be the same.

Jerry Kramer was a member of the Packers' offensive line from 1958 to 1968. During that time, Green Bay won five NFL titles, including the first two Super Bowls.

Jerry Kramer (64) clears a path for running back Elijah Pitts (22) during Super Bowl I. The Packers defeated the Chiefs 35–10.

Today, the Packers are the embodiment of the NFL—what it was and what it should be. They have the longest continuous residence in a single town in NFL history, and they own 13 NFL titles, including four Super Bowl championships. The team's history is studded with players who are among the best ever—guys like Don Hutson, "Iron Mike" Michalske, Arnie Herber, Cal Hubbard, Curly Lambeau, Tony Canadeo, Henry Jordan, Ray Nitschke, Jim Taylor, Paul Hornung, Fuzzy Thurston, Herb Adderley, Willie Davis, Willie Wood, James Lofton, Reggie White, and, of course, Brett Favre.

These players made the NFL special, and they helped to make the Super Bowl the most-watched annual sporting event in the world. They are also the reason so many fans consider Lambeau Field to be a shrine—they believe it's the cornerstone of the NFL.

To be a Green Bay Packer is to understand and embrace the team's unique history. The players of today know what they owe to the players of the past, and most are honored to be a part of this legendary franchise. Today's players still want to know all about Coach Lombardi and how cold the Ice Bowl game really was (the windchill was –57 degrees at game's end).

That's what makes *Green Bay Packers: Yesterday & Today*™ so special. It details the aura of the Packers from the team's humble beginnings all the way to the modern era. This book chronicles the players who made it all possible, as well as George Calhoun, the "Hungry Five," the stock sales, Hagemeister Park, Rockwood Lodge, the "Instant Replay Game," and the Monday Night epic against the Redskins. Mostly, it's an American tale about triumph and tragedy, failure and success, and everything in between.

It's been an honor for me to have been associated with the Packers for so many years, and it's a pleasure for me to be a part of a book that so richly depicts the team's history—a story that is still being written.

Jerry Kramer
#64

Jerry Kramer

CHAPTER ONE

HUMBLE BEGINNINGS

1919–1928

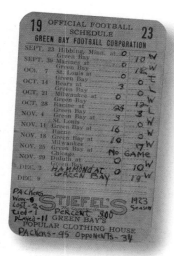

"Why not get up a team in Green Bay?"

PACKERS COFOUNDER GEORGE CALHOUN

Above: *Early on in the history of the franchise, fans knew they had something special in Green Bay, so they held on to mementos such as this schedule from 1923.* **Right:** *On October 14, 1923, the Chicago Bears made their first visit to Green Bay to face the Packers at Bellevue Park. Curly Lambeau (second from left) and the rest of the Pack played them tough, but the Bears prevailed 3–0.*

The Birth and Early Days of Green Bay Packers Football

There is as much myth as fact when it comes to the birth of the Green Bay Packers. The story, or at least the story most people like to relate, is how two larger-than-life figures—*Green Bay Press-Gazette* sports editor George Calhoun and local star athlete Earl Louis "Curly" Lambeau—met over a beer one night during the summer of 1919 to create what would become a legendary football team. It sounds nice, and, as with most stories, elements are true. But, over time, it became far more complicated than that, and a lot more interesting.

The Packers, or what would eventually become the Packers, were born in bits and pieces, cobbled together and molded by perfect timing and luck and talent. That was the starting point for the Packers, but Green Bay had loved football for years before Lambeau and Calhoun decided to meet. And no one was a bigger fan than a young Lambeau, who, as a kid, had attended games at Hagemeister Park, watching a collection of locals take on teams from around the area.

Lambeau was a gifted player in his own right, first leading Green Bay East High School and then attending the University of Wisconsin in Madison, where he left after barely a month because the freshman football program was canceled, and he wasn't allowed to play on the varsity. In the interim, Lambeau returned to Green Bay, worked construction for his father, and played for a team called the South Side Skiddoos.

But the idea of the Packers may have started brewing in Lambeau's head while he was playing alongside George Gipp at Notre Dame for the legendary Knute Rockne. When a severe case of tonsillitis sent Lambeau back home to recuperate, he applied for a job at the Indian Packing Corporation, which had recently moved to town.

In August of 1919, sports editor George Calhoun, seen here at his desk at the Green Bay Press-Gazette, *met with Curly Lambeau to discuss the idea of starting a professional football team in Green Bay.*

FOOTBALL PLAYERS CALLED FOR MEET ON FRIDAY NIGHT

Indian Packing Corporation Squad to Gather at Press-Gazette at 7:45..

Footballers on the Indian Packing Corporation squad will hold an important meeting in the editorial rooms of The Press-Gazette on Friday evening at 7:45. It is of utmost importance that every man be on hand as final plans for the season will be outlined.

The footballers will hold their first practice on Sept. 3, the Wednesday after Labor Day. Negotiations have been practically completed for the opening game on Sunday, Sept. 14.

The uniforms, which are being furnished by the Indian Packing Corporation, will be here in time for the opening game and the "Packers" will be outfitted in college style.

Many of the best teams in the state want to be seen in action here this season. Inquiries about games have been received from Milwaukee, Racine, Kenosha, Waukesha, La Crosse, and Madison. Marinette, Menominee, Oconto, Oshkosh and Appleton will play in Green Bay during the fore part of the season.

This August 1919 article from the Green Bay Press-Gazette *was a callout to anyone interested in playing for the town's newest football team, soon to be known as the Packers.*

Earl "Curly" Lambeau cofounded the Green Bay Packers along with George Calhoun in 1919. Lambeau was also the team's first coach and quarterback.

Frank Peck, a company executive who knew Lambeau's name from his exploits at Notre Dame, hired him as traffic manager for the then-staggering sum of $250 per month. But Lambeau wasn't finished with football, and, in 1919, he and Calhoun met at a local tavern to talk about forming a team.

It wasn't an especially dramatic meeting, despite what legend suggests. But it did serve a key function in that Calhoun convinced Lambeau to stay in Green Bay rather than return to Notre Dame for another year.

Lambeau would be the star player and Calhoun would take the reins as team manager, extolling the wonders of football every day in the pages of the *Press-Gazette,* in pieces such as this one:

> "'Curly' Lambeau, former East High and Notre Dame star, was elected captain of the Indian Packing Corporation's team at a meeting last night of the city footballers in the Press-Gazette....
>
> Close to 25 pigskin chasers attended the conference last evening and there was a good deal of enthusiasm displayed among the candidates. It was the unanimous opinion that, if Green Bay doesn't get away with state honors this year she never will."

Packermania had begun.

The Name Game

It just wouldn't be the same if they were the Green Bay Indians. Or the Bays. Or the Blues. Or, perhaps, the Big Bay Blue Boys?

But the Green Bay Packers weren't always called the Packers, and if Curly Lambeau had his way, they never would have been.

Indeed, no one involved with the fledgling club was happy with any of the names suggested for the team in the early days. George Calhoun and Lambeau both despised the name Packers, and Lambeau cringed when Calhoun routinely referred to the team as the Big Bay Blue Boys in his articles.

Indians was a logical choice and also a nod to the Indian Packing Corporation, which sponsored the team and kept it alive for the first few years. The name Blues came from the team colors (which were picked up from Notre Dame). In the end, though, thanks to the $500 put up by Frank Peck and the sponsoring Indian Packing Corporation, the name everyone settled on was the Packers. And that name has been indelibly carved into the American sports landscape.

This painting depicts Curly Lambeau in his Packers uniform. The blue and gold team colors were a tribute to Notre Dame.

Leader of the Pack

Early on, Earl Louis "Curly" Lambeau knew he was destined for great things. But even though he was a star football player growing up—first at Whitney Grade School and then at Green Bay East High School—Lambeau never had an inkling that he would help form a professional football team in his hometown, take it to the heights of success, and eventually earn a hallowed spot in the sport's Hall of Fame. Still, as a kid, he never lacked confidence.

Indeed, under his high school yearbook senior photo, Lambeau's defining statement said simply, "When I get through with athletics, I'm going out and conquer the rest of the world."

In high school, Lambeau was a one-of-a-kind athlete. Taller, stronger, and simply better than the kids he competed against, he not only excelled at football (where he was a great runner, passer, and kicker), he was also captain of the East High track team, where he won state titles in the shot put, hammer throw, long jump, and discus throw.

But football was clearly Lambeau's first love, and in 1918, after saving up enough money from working at his father's construction firm over the summer, Lambeau enrolled at Notre Dame to play for a new coach named Knute Rockne.

Lambeau quickly became Notre Dame's starting fullback and scored the first touchdown of his college career—and the first touchdown of the Rockne era—in a 26–6 win over the Case School of Applied Science.

Lambeau played fullback and halfback and scored three touchdowns for the Fighting Irish, who had a 3–1–2 record in 1918. And while Rockne saw big things ahead for his young star, fate would intervene. An illness sent Lambeau back to Green Bay during the winter, and his college career was sidetracked when he took a job at the Indian Packing Corporation in Green Bay.

Everything was changing, and soon, through Lambeau's determination and grit, a team known as the Green Bay Packers would be born.

Curly Lambeau started the Packers in 1919 and served as both head coach and quarterback for the team until 1929, when he moved to the sidelines full-time.

Curly Lambeau's birthplace, seen here in 2009, sits on Irwin Street in Green Bay.

The First Season

It was one thing to put a team together. But as Curly Lambeau and George Calhoun would quickly discover, finding opponents willing to take on this powerful bunch was another matter entirely. This was not the NFL that would eventually develop conferences and predetermined opponents—this was football in its rawest, most nomadic form. Find a collection of players, decide on a day, a time, and a place, and then go play.

And so, in 1919, the newly christened Green Bay Packers played teams in Milwaukee and Chicago, as well as teams in Marinette, Sheboygan, and New London, a small town west of Green Bay. Lambeau also arranged games with teams from the gritty iron ore towns in the Upper Peninsula of Michigan.

That first season, the Packers played ten games and rolled over everyone they took on, outscoring the opposition 565–6. But along the way, in a brutal game against Ishpeming, the Packers ran the ball on their first three plays, and each time, a player suffered a broken bone. Lambeau recalled later, "We never ran again. We passed on every play and we beat them 33–0. It was the day we realized the value of the forward pass."

During the final game of the season—the unofficial "state championship"—the Packers faced the Beloit Fairies. Beloit's 6–0 victory was controversial, to say the least, because referee Baldy Zabel disallowed Packers touchdowns on three straight plays at the end of the game.

Not surprisingly, the sports pages of the *Green Bay Press-Gazette* sizzled afterward. "Capt. Lambeau's team was robbed of victory by referee Zabel of Beloit," Calhoun wrote. "This official penalized Green Bay three times after touchdowns, refusing to allow the score. The Packers were twice on the verge of leaving the field but decided to play it out."

Furious, Calhoun demanded a rematch on a neutral field with neutral officials, but Beloit refused. No wonder the team was called the Fairies, Calhoun joked.

Still, a 10–1 inaugural season was nothing to complain about.

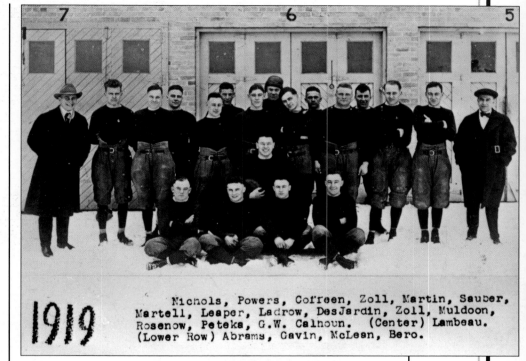

Nichols, Powers, Coffeen, Zoll, Martin, Sauber, Martell, Leaper, Ladrow, DesJardin, Zoll, Muldoon, Rosenow, Peteka, G.W. Calhoun. (Center) Lambeau. (Lower Row) Abrams, Gavin, McLean, Bero.

1919

Only two teams were able to score against the 1919 Green Bay Packers, who went 10–1 in their first season in existence. Their only loss came in a controversial 6–0 defeat at the hands of the Beloit Fairies. In this photo, Curly Lambeau (center) sports a wide grin and holds a football.

Passing the Hat

For their efforts that first season, the 21 players remaining on the team split the gate receipts—money from ticket sales and anything the team could cajole from fans in the stands. Indeed, at every home game, a hat was passed around to spectators, who were asked to give what they could to keep the team going. At season's end, after Calhoun totaled up all the money that was left, each player received $16.75, which equaled about three days' pay from their regular jobs.

Game Day

They had to play somewhere. And for the fledgling Green Bay Packers, the first, best, and really only choice for a home turf was Hagemeister Park.

Since the early 1900s, Hagemeister Park had been used for football games in Green Bay, but it was really nothing more than a grass field near East High School. There were no grandstands or bleachers. There were no ushers. There were no concession stands. And there was no public address system or scoreboard.

It was community football in every sense of the word, as fans could jump off the streetcar on nearby Walnut Street and walk up to the roped-off area that separated the spectators from the field. Fans who drove to the game could park their cars and join the rest of the crowd.

At halftime, because there were no dressing rooms, the two teams would adjourn to opposite end zones to talk about second-half strategy. And, as always, a hat was passed around so fans could contribute to the Packers' effort.

By 1920, some grandstands had been built to seat a few hundred people, and starting in 1921, admission was charged. When Hagemeister Park was torn down in 1923, so the city's new East High School could be built, the Packers took their show to Bellevue Park, a minor league baseball field that seated around 4,000 people.

The Packers played at Bellevue Park until 1925, and it was during those years that the team's popularity really began to take off. But the park was

Red Dunn carries the ball in this photo from the October 14, 1928, game against the Chicago Cardinals. The Packers routed the Cards 20–0.

located in the northeastern part of town, so it was difficult for fans, most of whom still lived closer to downtown Green Bay, to get there via public transportation.

As a result, team officials coordinated with the city and the Green Bay school board to build a new stadium closer to where the Packers got their start. Behind the new East High School, a 6,000-seat ballpark called City Stadium would become the Packers new home starting in September 1925.

Horseshoe-shape and made entirely of wood, City Stadium still lacked many modern comforts, including toilet facilities. The Packers would dress in the high school locker room, while visiting teams usually dressed for games in their hotel rooms.

City Stadium was eventually expanded to seat 25,000 and served as the Packers' home until 1956, when a new City Stadium was built at the corner of Highland and Oneida. Eventually, that structure would be renamed Lambeau Field.

During the 1923 and '24 seasons, the Packers played at Bellevue Park. Hagemeister Park had been demolished so that City Stadium could be built.

The Packers Join the APFA

In their first two years of existence, the Green Bay Packers played just about anybody who wanted to play them. In 1919, the games came against teams from Marinette, Oshkosh, and Ishpeming. It wasn't much different in 1920, as the Packers went 9–1–1 and allowed just 24 points all season to teams from DePere, Kaukauna, and Menominee.

The game was changing, not only in Green Bay, but throughout the Midwest—a hotbed for football. George Halas, who had started a team called the Staleys in downstate Decatur, Illinois, had an idea to start a new league that would organize the franchises, set standards and rules, and offer the game opportunities to grow.

The league was called the American Professional Football Association (APFA), and it started in 1920 without Green Bay. Curly Lambeau wanted his Packers to be part of the organization, but it wouldn't be easy to gain admission to this tight fellowship.

The league already had more than a dozen teams, including two in Chicago and six in Ohio. Green Bay would be the smallest town with a franchise, and some teams had concerns about that. But on August 27, 1921, after several hours of negotiations and with the support of the owners of the Chicago Cardinals and Canton Bulldogs—two of the bigger teams in the league—brothers John and Emmitt Clair of the Acme Packing Company (which had recently bought out the Indian Packing Corporation and still sponsored the team) were granted a franchise for a pro team in Green Bay for a $50 fee.

The sensational news swept throughout Green Bay and the entire state, and Lambeau was able to start attracting players that would help his team compete in this new league. The best of the bunch was Howard "Cub" Buck, who signed a contract guaranteeing him $75 per game.

The team's first APFA matchup was on October 23, 1921, against the Minneapolis Marines at Hagemeister Park. The Marines had been one of the Midwest's top independent teams

GREEN BAY PACKERS-1920
TOP ROW— J. Delloy, Powers, Dwyer, Klaus, Nickols, Rosenow, Wilson, Sauber, Murphy, (coach).
MIDDLE ROW— H. Tebo, Petka, Gavin, Wheeler, Lambeau, (capt) Ladrow, Wagner, Dalton, Jonet.
BOTTOM ROW— M. Zoll, Leaper, C. Zoll, Martell, McClean, Abrams, Medley.

In 1920, the powerful Pack went 9–1–1, but they would not gain entrance into the APFA until the following season.

and were also new members of the league. Green Bay won its first league game 7–6 in front of 6,000 fans.

That season, the Packers also beat teams from Evansville and Hammond, Indiana, but on November 27, they lost to the Chicago Staleys (who would later become the Chicago Bears). It was the start of a rivalry that burns just as hot today.

The Packers finished 3–2–1 in 1921, but the foundation had been set. The APFA was renamed the National Football League in 1922, and in those early days, teams came and went in a flurry. But not the Green Bay Packers. Of the original members of the APFA/NFL, the Packers are the only team that is still using the same name and residing in the same city.

Speed Bump

It seemed like a good idea at the time. Besides, in 1921, in the slightly shadowy world of the American Professional Football Association—where rules were really more like suggestions—the Green Bay Packers were only doing what other teams could and would do if given the opportunity.

Still, as the Packers and Curly Lambeau faced the first real disaster of their professional lives, the irony could not be ignored. Here was Lambeau, who had played for the legendary Knute Rockne at Notre Dame, facing the potential end of his professional football career *because of* Notre Dame and Rockne.

In late November 1921, during their first season in the APFA, the Packers traveled to Chicago to face the Staleys. The college football season was over, and while most collegians used that time to heal up and focus on their studies, there were a dedicated few who wanted to keep playing and, perhaps, pick up a few bucks in the process. That's what happened in Chicago, as three Notre Dame players put on Packers uniforms to play the Staleys.

Unbeknownst to Lambeau, several Chicago sportswriters in attendance recognized one of the Notre Dame players—Heartley

In 1921, when Heartly "Hunk" Anderson (seen here on the right with Fighting Irish coach Knute Rockne) suited up for Green Bay, along with two other Notre Dame players, it nearly meant the end of the Packers.

The 1921 season was Green Bay's third year with a professional football team, and due to a scandal involving the use of illegal players, it was almost the last.

"Hunk" Anderson—and the jig was up. Rockne found out and suspended the players, and when the other APFA teams were informed, Green Bay had its franchise revoked for the 1922 season.

Even today, there is no hard evidence that the three collegians actually played for the Packers, but the perception was all that was needed. Green Bay was in it deep.

Lambeau acted swiftly and decisively. First, he did something that was completely against his nature—he swallowed his pride, apologized to the league, and asked that the franchise be reinstated. In the meantime, Emmitt Clair relinquished his claim to the franchise, so Lambeau saw this as an opportunity to solidify the team in Green Bay by buying it back.

Twice, Lambeau had to apply to the league for reinstatement. After pleading his case to the league, Lambeau was finally able to shell out $50 of his own money to get Green Bay's franchise reinstated on June 24, 1922. The Packers were back in business, but it had been a long, expensive process. Now it was time to find players, put a schedule together, and get back to football. But even that would prove to be no easy feat.

The Bears–Packers Rivalry

The longest-running continuous rivalry in pro football began on a cold November afternoon in 1921.

At the time, it was just another game between two rugged midwestern teams in the brand-new American Professional Football Association. But it also featured two men with enormous talent and even bigger egos, and it would start one of the greatest rivalries in sports.

George Halas and Curly Lambeau got their starts in similar fashions. Both were hard-bitten midwesterners, and both were obsessed with football and starred at the sport during their high school and college days.

But Halas had a vision that Lambeau didn't necessarily possess. Halas saw pro football as the next great American game, and he took the first steps toward proving it by helping to form the APFA in 1920 in Canton, Ohio. Naturally, his newly formed football team, the Decatur Staleys, would be part of it.

When the Packers joined the league in 1921, it was initially thought that the Minneapolis Marines might end up being their natural geographic rival. Instead, on November 27, 1921, Lambeau and the Packers and Halas's team, now called the Chicago Staleys, met for the first time. They have battled at least once every season since.

The Packers readily agreed to take the train south to Chicago—and they brought more than 300 Packer Backers with them on the special excursion.

With Lambeau at quarterback and Halas playing right end, the Packers lost that first meeting with the Staleys 20–0. But it hardly mattered to Packers fans, who enjoyed themselves thoroughly in the big city.

The following season, the APFA was renamed the National Football League. And the Staleys, who had been named after the food processing company in downstate Illinois that had funded Halas's new team, were renamed the Bears.

The Packers and the Bears have been at war ever since.

The bitter rivalry between the Packers and the Bears, which began way back in 1921, has been going strong ever since, as these mementos clearly demonstrate.

And So It Begins...

You needn't dig too far or too deep to find the seeds of what would become the Bears–Packers rivalry. Indeed, it began in the very first meeting between the two teams, when Chicago's John "Tarzan" Taylor hit Packers star Howard "Cub" Buck in the face and broke his nose.

Taylor's audacity was impressive, since he stood just 5'11" and weighed 175 pounds, while Buck, the Packers' highest-paid player, stood tall at 6'3" and 250 pounds.

But Buck, who worked as the executive director of the Boy Scouts of America in nearby Appleton, refused to retaliate. Instead, he lectured Taylor, saying, "You are supposed to be a college graduate and a gentleman, you know."

The Hungry Five

For the still struggling Green Bay Packers, their first years in existence had taken a toll.

It was the team's first season back after its franchise had been suspended for using illegal players. Then, midway through the 1922 season, the Packers saw their future literally hinge on .01 inch of rain that *didn't* fall in a November game against Columbus. The team had taken out an insurance policy, which stated that if bad weather held down home crowds, the team could recover its financial losses.

So Green Bay played in the driving rain, the crowd was scant, and the Packers went to make their claim only to be told that the rainfall wasn't sufficient to activate the policy. The Packers lost thousands of dollars they couldn't afford to lose.

But this incident led to the 1923 formation of a local group called the "Hungry Five," which not only kept the Packers'

franchise alive but also put it on the road to solvency. The group included Lambeau—the heart and soul of the Packers—as well as four other solid members of the community, who each brought a special skill that helped keep the Packers' organization functioning.

The group included *Green Bay Press-Gazette* general manager A. B. Turnbull, a longtime backer of the Packers who knew how to raise money; Lee Joannes, a local grocer; Gerald Clifford, a razor-sharp attorney; and Dr. W. Webber Kelly, a top-notch physician.

Their job was simple: find money to keep the franchise going. Cajole, wheedle, beg, threaten—it really didn't matter. So effective were they that *Milwaukee Journal* sportswriter Oliver Kuechle nicknamed them "The Hungry Five." The five did not discourage the moniker.

In the early days of Green Bay Packers history, money was tight and the club almost folded for financial reasons on several occasions. Thanks in part to a group of local businessmen, who along with Curly Lambeau were known as "The Hungry Five," the Green Bay Packers stayed afloat. "The Hungry Five" were (from left to right): A. B. Turnbull, Gerald Clifford, Curly Lambeau, Dr. W. Webber Kelly, and Lee Joannes.

On the Verge of Greatness

Call it the calm before the storm. For four seasons, the Green Bay Packers had grimly hung on both financially and competitively, first as part of the American Professional Football Association and then in the National Football League. They had survived a potentially disastrous illegal player scandal, which saw the loss of the team's franchise and required a humiliating admission of guilt. The team had struggled financially, which led to the formation of "The Hungry Five" and routine trips through the stands to collect money from the crowd. And they had already played in two ballparks, neither of which was adequate.

But the Packers persevered and actually flourished under the most trying of circumstances. And by 1925, they were making money, filling the stands, and winning games.

That same year, the Packers opened the first real stadium built just for them. In conjunction with the city of Green Bay and the local school board, the Packers built a new 6,000-seat stadium adjacent to the site of their first home, the former Hagemeister Park. Known as City Stadium, the new facility opened on September 20, 1925, as the Packers faced off against the Hammond Pros in front of 3,000 fans.

With their financial concerns seemingly under control, the Packers spent the next few years building a strong fan base and developing a team that would soon become what was perhaps the NFL's first dominant team.

From 1925 to 1928, the Packers, with Curly Lambeau still firmly in control, put key pieces of the puzzle together on the field: Lavvie Dilweg was the star offensive end; Verne Lewellen was the leading rusher; Bernard "Boob" Darling and "Jug" Earp dominated the offensive line; and Joseph "Red" Dunn was a valuable all-purpose back. In that four-year stretch, the Packers posted a 28–14–7 record.

Perhaps most importantly, on September 27, 1925, in front of nearly 6,000 fans at City Stadium, the Packers beat the Chicago Bears for the first time in four tries.

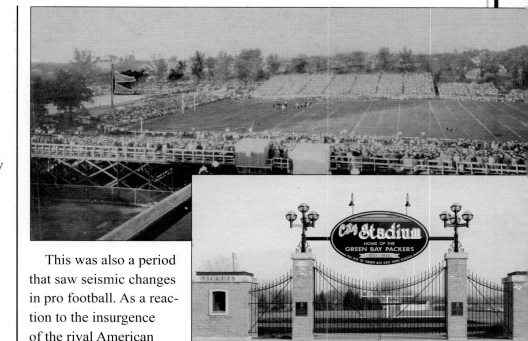

City Stadium—yesterday and today. Seen here in the 1930s (above) and in 2009, City Stadium was the home of the Green Bay Packers from 1925 until 1956, and now serves as the home turf of Green Bay East High School's Red Devils.

This was also a period that saw seismic changes in pro football. As a reaction to the insurgence of the rival American Football League (AFL) in 1926, the NFL increased its membership to 22 teams. But by 1927, the AFL was already history, and the NFL was back down to 12 teams.

The Packers went 7–2–1 in 1927, with their only two losses coming at the hands of the Bears. In 1928, Green Bay finished 6–4–3.

It was during the off-season between 1928 and 1929 when Lambeau—ever the salesman—convinced three players who had struggled with other NFL teams to come to Green Bay. They were August "Iron Mike" Michalske, Robert "Cal" Hubbard, and Johnny (Blood) McNally. And they would help take the Packers where they had never gone before.

Stars of the Era

Perhaps the Packers' first real "pro," **Howard "Cub" Buck** joined the Packers as a tackle in 1921 for the princely sum of $75 per game. He'd been an outstanding guard at the University of Wisconsin and had played one season for the Canton Bulldogs, where he blocked for the game's best player at the time, Jim Thorpe. At 6'3" and 250 pounds, Buck was one of the biggest players in the game. He retired in 1926 to become head football coach at the University of Miami in Florida and was inducted into the Packers Hall of Fame in 1977.

Louis "Jug" Earp's nickname was originally "Juggernaut," which was then shortened to "Jugger," and finally to "Jug." Earp joined the Packers in 1922 after starting the season with the Rock Island Independents, a team based on the Illinois–Iowa border. But that club grew tired of his constant arguing, so when Lambeau asked about the lineman's availability, Rock Island gladly sent him over. Earp—a distant relative of lawman Wyatt Earp—played 11 seasons with the Packers and, at 6'1" and 235 pounds, was considered one of the best defensive tackles of the Lambeau era. He was named to the Packers Hall of Fame in 1970.

During his time with the Packers, Howard "Cub" Buck also worked as an executive with the Boy Scouts of America.

One of the toughest players of the Packers' early days, Louis "Jug" Earp often played despite painful injuries. He was known to play with broken ribs and an arm so badly injured that he could barely lift it.

Verne Lewellen had been a star halfback at the University of Nebraska, but when he signed with the Packers in 1924, he became the team's first high-profile running back, rushing for 37 touchdowns in nine seasons. Lewellen was elected Brown County District Attorney in 1929, while he was still playing for the Packers. He retired from football after the 1932 season, later served as the Packers' general manager, and was inducted into the Packers Hall of Fame in 1970.

Considered the Packers' best two-way end—at least until Don Hutson came onto the scene—**Lavern "Lavvie" Dilweg** played at Marquette University and played professionally for the Milwaukee Badgers until that franchise folded. He joined the Packers in 1927 and scored 12 touchdowns for the team from 1927 to 1934. He later served in Congress from 1943 to 1945, and his grandson, quarterback Anthony Dilweg, played for the Packers from 1989 to 1990. Lavvie Dilweg was inducted into the Packers Hall of Fame in 1970.

One of the best ends in the game during his time, Lavvie Dilweg make a second career for himself practicing law and later served a term in Congress.

Verne Lewellen was known for kicking towering punts 50–60 yards. He later served as the Packers' first general manager from 1954 to 1957.

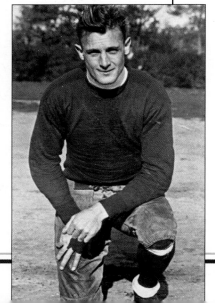

Bernard "Boob" Darling joined the Packers as a center in 1927 and became a mainstay on the team's offensive line for five seasons. He later served on the Packers' Board of Directors and Executive Committee during the 1950s and was elected to the Packers Hall of Fame in 1970, two years after his death.

Although he's seldom mentioned among the early icons of Packers history, **Bo Molenda** was nonetheless an important acquisition at a key time for the franchise.

After starring at fullback at the University of Michigan, Molenda played football professionally with the New York Yankees for a season and a half. But midway through the 1928 season, the Packers purchased his contract, and local papers touted Molenda as one of the best fullbacks in the NFL.

With the ability to play both offense and defense, Molenda played nearly every minute of every game and was a key contributor to Green Bay winning three straight NFL titles from 1929 to 1931. He even served as the Packers' kicker during that time.

Molenda left the Packers during the 1932 season and retired as a member of the New York Giants after the 1935 season. He eventually returned to Green Bay as an assistant coach under Curly Lambeau during the 1947 and '48 seasons.

Above: Bernard "Boob" Darling was a star center at Beloit College before joining the Packers in 1927. Below: Bo Molenda was a sparkplug on the Packers teams that won three straight NFL titles.

The Green Bay Packers held their first stock sale at a local Elks Club in August 1923. They sold 1,000 shares at $5 apiece to get the team out of financial peril.

Turning a Profit

In early 1923, Curly Lambeau and the Green Bay Packers were $2,500 in debt. But by August, the organization that had gotten off to such a fitful start professionally had found the answer: The Packers would sell stock in the franchise for $5 a share. In addition, the team was playing well enough on the field that attendance was increasing.

At the annual stockholders meeting in January 1925, A. B. Turnbull announced that the Packers had paid off all their debts. Those $5 shares of stock purchased by community members were enough to get the Packers out of debt and also provided a way to keep the franchise solvent down the road. As evidence, Turnbull said the Packers had even turned a profit that season. The amount? $2.20.

PACKERS PARAPHERNALIA

On November 2, 1924, the Green Bay Packers took on the Racine Legion at Bellevue Park. The Pack was victorious by a score of 6-3.

GREEN BAY FOOTBALL CORPORATION

OFFICIAL PROGRAM — SUNDAY, NOVEMBER 2
Green Bay Packers VS. **Racine Legion**

The games played at home by the Packers, the Green Bay Football corporation's team, are for the benefit of the Sullivan Post of the American Legion.

| Sunday, Nov. 9 LAST HOME GAME Sunday Nov. 9 | Green Bay Packers vs. Duluth Kellys NORTHWEST CHAMPIONSHIP GAME PRICES $1.00-$1.50 KICK OFF 2:00 | Sunday, Nov. 9 LAST HOME GAME Sunday, Nov. 9 |

This contract shows that fullback Arthur Schmaehl was paid $50 per game to play for the Packers during the 1921 season, his only season in the NFL. He played in six games and scored two touchdowns.

The American Professional Football Association
UNIFORM PLAYER'S CONTRACT

GREEN BAY PACKERS-1923
FIRST ROW — Lambeau, Murray, Earps, Gardner, Nieman, Buck, Basing, Carey.
SECOND ROW — Woodin, Hayes, Gavin, Mathys, Mills, Wheeler, Lyle.

In addition to Curly Lambeau, Jug Earp, and Cub Buck, several other players on the Packers' 1923 squad had flashy nicknames, such as Jab Murray, Moose Gardner, Whitey Woodin, Buck Gavin, and Cowboy Wheeler.

GREEN BAY "PACKERS"-1924
FIRST ROW — Buck, O'Donnell, Lambeau, Woodin, Earps,
SECOND ROW — Gardner, Hendrian, Hearnden, Mathys, Murray, Basing,
THIRD ROW — Rosatti, Nieman, Voss, Lewellen, Duford.

The 1924 Packers finished sixth in the league with a record of 7-4, but there were some stars on the roster, including Cub Buck, Curly Lambeau, Jug Earp, and Verne Lewellen.

GREEN BAY FOOTBALL CORPORATION

OFFICIAL PROGRAM   **SUNDAY, SEPTEMBER 14**

Green Bay Packers   vs.   Ironwood Legion

The games played at home by the Packers, the Green Bay Football corporation's team, are for the benefit of the Sullivan Post of the American Legion.

| Sunday, Sept. 21 NEXT HOME GAME Sunday, Sept. 21 | Green Bay Packers vs. Chicago Bears One of the Season's Big Games PRICES $1.00–$1.50   KICK OFF 2:30 | Sunday, Sept. 21 NEXT HOME GAME Sunday, Sept. 21 |

GREEN BAY PACKERS

No.	Player	College	Weight	Position
4	O'DONNELL	Minn.	180	END
5	MILTON	Cal.	178	END
10	BUCK	Wis.	265	TACKLE
7	WOODIN	Marq.	210	GUARD
12	NIEMAN	Mich.	190	CENTER
14	BULAND	Syra.	205	GUARD
6	EARPS	Mon.	220	TACKLE
16	ROSSATTI	Mich.	212	TACKLE
7	VOSS	Del.	205	END
13	HEARNDEN	St. A.	175	END
2	MATHYS	Ind.	170	QUARTER BACK
15	LEWELLEN	Neb.	185	HALF BACK
6	HENDRIAN	Prin.	180	FULL BACK
1	LAMBEAU	N. D.	190	HALF BACK
18	BEASEY	S. D.	162	FULL BACK
11	BASING	Law.	190	HALF BACK
8	GARDNER	Wis.	205	GUARD
17	LUDTKE	Kan.	192	GUARD

IRONWOOD LEGION

Player	College	Weight	No.
BENTON	Mich.	190	31
HARRINGTON	St. Nor.	170	6
HELL	W. A. C.	185	29
CAULDWELL	Val.	235	12
DENFIELD	Navy	200	17
RITZ	But.	205	17
BEAR	Iowa	185	16
GARSICH	Iowa	217	8
MARSHALL	Minn.	200	4
DONALD	Minn.	185	28
HOLMAN	St. P.	185	2
MASON	Minn.	185	7
EAGLEBURGER	Wis.	160	25
SANDERSON	Wis.	155	18
LARINSON	Mich.	160	1
HARRIS	N. D.	190	11
NADOLNY	Syra.	230	4
EADON	Mich.	198	5

Referee, Coffeen; Umpire, White; Head Linesman, Wiley; Time of periods, 12 minutes.
Kick off, 2:30 sharp.

KEEP EVRARD YOUR DISTRICT ATTORNEY ELECTION

Saxe's Strand
GLORIA SWANSON in "MANHANDLED"
NOW PLAYING
STRAND SUPERIOR ORCHESTRA

A program from a 1924 game against the Ironwood Legion notes that Packers home games benefit the Sullivan Post of the American Legion.

The Packers of the mid-1920s were hardly spectacular, finishing in sixth place in 1924, ninth in '25, and fifth in '26. But fans preserved every memory for posterity.

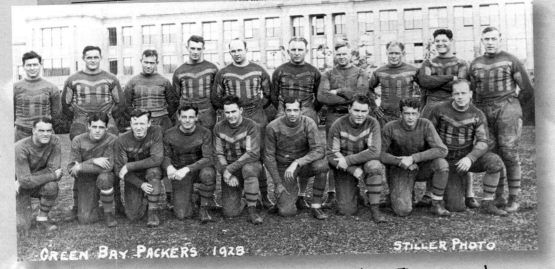

GREEN BAY PACKERS 1928   STILLER PHOTO

The 1928 Packers, who finished fourth in the NFL, were only a year away from their first title. Stars such as Curly Lambeau (top left), Lavvie Dilweg (top row, fourth from left), Jug Earp (top right), and Boob Darling (bottom row, second from right) would lead them there.

WISCONSIN PROFESSIONAL CHAMPIONS SINCE 1917

Green Bay Football Club
(Formerly Packers)
Members National Football League
GREEN BAY, WIS.

EXECUTIVES
E. L. Lambeau
Nathan Abrams
G. W. Calhoun

Phone 4400

Sept. 3, 1924

T. Edward Sullivan
Fond du Lac, Wis.

Dear Sir:

    I glimpsed an article in one of your Fond Du Lac papers regarding giving plans on your Armistice Day celebration and mentioning the fact that it was possible that you would stage a professional football game on that date.

    It is quite possible that the Green Bay Packers management might be very much interested in the proposition. As champions of the Northwest, I think we are entitled to first consideration by your associates.

    I am writing this letter in the absence of A. B. Turnbull, our club president, who is vacationing in Michigan. I would suggest that if the newspaper story is authentic, it might be a good idea for you to get in touch with us about the game.

    Anticipating an early reply hoping that the negotiations may climax satisfactorily, I remain,

Yours Very Truly,
GREEN BAY FOOTBALL CORPORATION

In this letter from 1924, George Calhoun graciously volunteers the Packers—the "champions of the Northwest"—to play in a game held in Fond du Lac during an Armistice Day celebration.

CHAPTER TWO

BUILDING A DYNASTY

1929–1949

"When a city responds as it has done to our efforts,
I'll say it certainly deserves a championship."

CURLY LAMBEAU

Above: *Helmets like this one, which belonged to Paul "Tiny" Engebretsen, were worn by Packers players in the late 1930s.* **Right:** *The Green Bay Packers celebrate the club's sixth NFL title after defeating the New York Giants 14–7 in the 1944 championship game at the Polo Grounds.*

Three-Peat

In one respect, pro football of the late 1920s wasn't much different from its modern-day counterpart. Just as it is now, it was about improving the team from one year to the next, and to do that, management had to go out and find the best players possible.

Curly Lambeau obviously understood this, so after a 6–4–3 season in 1928, he thought the Packers could be on the verge of something special if they could just find the right pieces. He found them during the off-season with three players who would become among the best in the game.

The acquisitions of running back Johnny McNally and linemen Cal Hubbard and August "Iron Mike" Michalske helped lead the Packers to three straight NFL titles from 1929 to 1931.

McNally was the first key acquisition. A native of tiny New Richmond, Wisconsin, McNally may have been pro football's first true "free spirit." He played at a couple of colleges, including Notre Dame, but his love of football came at a price—literally.

This newspaper cartoon trumpets the fact that the Packers won three straight NFL championships from 1929 to 1931.

Somewhat of a football mercenary, McNally played for pay in places such as Milwaukee, Duluth, and Pottsville, Pennsylvania. And as teams learned of his vagabond nature, he realized that he couldn't play under his real name.

The story goes that McNally and a buddy saw the title of the Rudolph Valentino film *Blood and Sand* on a marquee while passing a movie house. McNally told his friend that they should use false names so they could play wherever they wanted without getting caught. "You be Sand," he told his friend, "and I'll be Blood." And so, Johnny Blood was born.

Michalske was next. A strong, quick lineman on both offense and defense, Michalske labored with the New York Yankees of the American Football League for two years before Lambeau lured him to Green Bay.

Then came Hubbard. He'd started his career with the New York Giants, but he had issues with the franchise. So when the opportunity to play in Green Bay came along, he grabbed it.

With all these pieces in place, the Packers glided through the 1929 season, outscoring their opponents 198–22 in 13 games. The only blemish on their record was a scoreless tie with Philadelphia's Frankford Yellow Jackets, in which the Packers swore they were shortchanged time on the clock, which might have cost them a score—and a win.

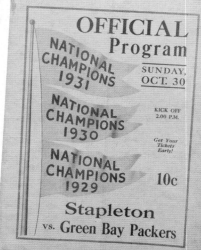

Programs like this one from a 1932 game against the Staten Island Stapletons remind fans of the Pack's first three-peat.

The Great Depression plummeted the global economy in 1929, but that didn't stop the Green Bay Packers from steamrolling opponents on the way to their first of three straight world championships.

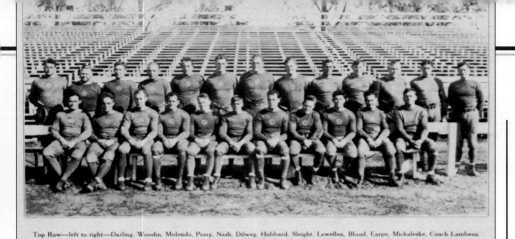

Top Row—left to right—Darling, Woodin, Molenda, Perry, Nash, Dilweg, Hubbard, Sleight, Lewellen, Blood, Earpe, Michaleske, Coach Lambeau.
Bottom Row—Bowdoin, Radick, Englemann, McCrary, Dunn, Zuildmulder, Zuver, Fitzgibbon, Herber, O'Donnell, Lidberg.

The 1930 Packers were not quite as unstoppable as the '29 squad, but they still managed to secure their second straight NFL championship.

Still, Green Bay wrapped up its first NFL title in the only way that seemed to make sense—with a 25–0 shutout of the Chicago Bears to complete a 12–0–1 season. It was, however, a championship in name only since the NFL would not hold its first title game until 1933. Nevertheless, the Packers had the best record, and, as such, they were the champs.

The Packers continued to evolve in 1930. The biggest change came at quarterback after Green Bay native Arnie Herber, who had grown up idolizing the Packers, was given a tryout by Lambeau. The coach was so impressed that he signed Herber for $75 per game, and Herber went on to become one of the greatest quarterbacks in team history.

The Pack ripped off eight straight wins to start the 1930 season before suffering back-to-back losses to the Chicago Cardinals and New York Giants. The Packers sputtered to the finish line with a loss to the Bears and a tie with Portsmouth (Ohio), but their 10–3–1 record was just good enough to edge the Giants for Green Bay's second straight NFL title.

In 1931, the Packers posted a 12–2 record, losing only to the Bears and Cardinals. They won the NFL title once again, but only after a controversy with Portsmouth was resolved by league president Joe Carr. Portsmouth, a team that was also battling for the title, said the Packers had verbally agreed to play them that season, but the game never took place. Carr ruled in favor of the Packers, giving Green Bay another title. But changes were looming on the horizon.

At the Top and Looking Down

By the early 1930s, Curly Lambeau was on top of the mountain. It had been barely a decade since he and George Calhoun had hatched the idea of founding a professional football franchise in tiny Green Bay. The Packers had survived financial troubles and controversy to become the first team to win three consecutive NFL championships. The team was loaded with future Hall of Famers and was the envy of the league. And Lambeau was its architect.

He'd been the team's first star player, but as the years went by, Lambeau knew that his role had to evolve. His playing days ended when he signed another Green Bay kid, Arnie Herber, to take over at quarterback starting in 1930. From that point on, Lambeau concentrated on coaching.

After the death of his mentor Knute Rockne in a plane crash in 1931, Lambeau was perhaps the most influential and recognizable coach in football thanks to his innovative use of the forward pass and the successful team he built in the little outpost of Green Bay.

But he was no joy to be around as a coach, at least for some of his players. Egotistical and stubborn, Lambeau had an attitude that rubbed some players the wrong way. "I never liked him," said Clarke Hinkle, a star back who joined the Packers in 1932. "I didn't really respect him either, but he was paying me, and I gave him a thousand percent every time I played football for him."

Then again, that's exactly what Lambeau demanded.

Trouble in the Stands

His name was Willard Bent, and he nearly put the Green Bay Packers out of business. An overexaggeration? Perhaps. But his lawsuit against the Packers in 1931 was yet another of the strange twists and turns that seemed to plague the franchise in its formative years.

It happened on September 20, 1931, during an otherwise nondescript 32–6 Packers thrashing of the Brooklyn Dodgers at City Stadium. In the second half, Bent, who later admitted that he was drunk, fell out of the stadium's bleachers and was injured. His injuries weren't life-threatening, but he filed a lawsuit against the Packers for $25,000—a sizable sum in those days.

The Packers didn't have that kind of money on hand, but the organization did have an insurance policy to handle what should have been little more than a nuisance. Two years later, Bent finally got his day in court and was awarded $5,200 in damages.

An incident at a September 1931 game caused quite a stir for the Packers.

Unfortunately for the Packers, during those two years, their insurance company had filed for bankruptcy. So not only did they not have the money to pay the judgment, they were also more than $12,000 in debt. A franchise that only a few years earlier had been one of the NFL's most financially stable was forced into receivership.

Once more, the "Hungry Five" rode to the rescue. One of the five, Green Bay grocery store magnate Leland Joannes, personally lent the team $6,000 to pay off half the debt. In addition, the court-appointed receiver, Frank Jonet, was a huge Packers fan, so he helped rearrange the remaining debt to make it more manageable. The Packers were even able to raise $15,000 in capital thanks to the public's response. Willard Bent was paid his settlement, and the Packers lived to play another day.

Home Away from Home

The Packers continued to draw well at City Stadium, but the facility had its limitations, both in terms of amenities and bleacher space. The Packers also knew that they needed to expand their fan base to avoid their seemingly endless financial woes. The answer was to play some of their home games in Milwaukee, the largest city in Wisconsin.

Fans in Green Bay, and Lambeau himself, were not happy about it, but on October 1, 1933, the Packers played their first game at Milwaukee's Borchert Field—a 10–7 loss to the New York Giants in front of nearly 13,000 fans. And so began a streak of 62 consecutive seasons in which the Packers played at least one game in Milwaukee. It ended in 1994 when, ironically, the same financial concerns that forced the team to start playing there caused them to stop. By the mid-1990s, the Packers were simply making more money playing at refurbished Lambeau Field than they were at cramped Milwaukee County Stadium. But to this day, Milwaukee fans are convinced that they're responsible for keeping the Packers alive. And they may well be right.

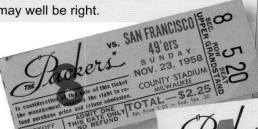

For more than sixty years, the Packers took their show on the road to play at least one game per season downstate in Milwaukee.

Green and Gold

By the start of the 1935 season, the Green Bay Packers needed something. A boost? A gimmick? A change of venue? Something.

The 1933 season had been a cold slap of reality—the team went 5–7–1, the club's first losing record since it became a pro franchise. The next year had been only marginally better, as the Packers had to win two of their last three games to fashion a winning record of 7–6. So Curly Lambeau, who was always on the lookout to make changes that mattered, made two of them.

Prior to the 1935 season, Lambeau decided to alter the team colors from dark blue and gold to green and gold. Make no mistake, this was more than just a frivolous cosmetic adjustment for the sake of change. Lambeau had originally made the team's colors blue and gold as a tribute to his old coach, Knute Rockne, and his old college, Notre Dame. But he had heard from more than a few fans that if the Packers were going to play in Green Bay, it might make sense to have green somewhere in the color scheme. Lambeau agreed.

And although green and gold didn't officially become the Packers' colors until the 1950s, the theme was set, and one of the most recognizable color schemes in sports was born.

But Lambeau wasn't finished making changes. It was also in 1935 that he instituted what would, in time, be known as "training camp." Other NFL teams had already been taking their players away to a camp prior to the start of the season to bond and practice

To prepare his team for the upcoming season, Curly Lambeau took his players to a wooded resort known as Pinewood Lodge, starting in 1935.

away from distractions. But the Packers had always been different. Traditionally, Lambeau would tell his players when to report for the start of the season, they'd show up, and off they'd go.

That summer, however, Lambeau decided that it was time for the Packers to have their own home away from home. So on August 24, 1935, the Packers gathered at Pinewood Lodge near Rhinelander, Wisconsin, deep in the northern woods about three hours from Green Bay. Golf and fishing were the only forms of recreation that Lambeau allowed his troops. Swimming in nearby Lake Thompson was forbidden, as was anything that involved alcohol. Lambeau was especially concerned about some of the summer residents in the resort area: It was reputed that many of Chicago's top mafia bosses vacationed by the lake, and the last thing Lambeau needed was to have some of his players cavorting with them.

This was no summer vacation or relaxing getaway for the Packers. It was all about football, and twice a day for two weeks, the team took a bus to Rhinelander High School to practice.

Training camp was now a part of the Packers' routine.

In 1935, after 15 years with a professional football team, Green Bay finally added green to its color scheme.

PACKERS PARAPHERNALIA

This Packers Bulletin previews an October 1930 game against the Frankford Yellow Jackets and notes a Thanksgiving Day contest between the two teams.

"Go! You Packers Go!", the team's fight song, was written by Milwaukee resident Eric Karll and was first played in 1931. The song is still played frequently during Packers home games.

This 1931 Bears-Packers game program points out that the Packers led the series 9-8-3 at the time by a combined score of 168-157.

On September 29, 1929, the Packers beat the Bears 23-0. They shut out their bitter rival two more times that season, scoring 62 unanswered points.

As this 1931 schedule shows, the Packers went 12–2 that year on their way to a third straight NFL title.

The Packers are hailed as world champs in this 1929 ad for Blue Ribbon Malt Extract, which could not be called beer because of Prohibition.

Between 1928 and 1932, Green Bay Packers Bulletins, like this one, were handed out free of charge to make fans aware of the team's next home game.

Helmets like the one pictured here were worn by the Green Bay Packers of the 1930s and '40s.

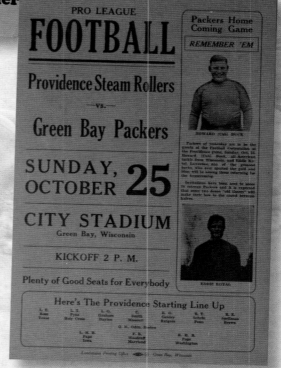

This Packers Bulletin from 1931 announces an upcoming game with Providence, whom Green Bay steamrolled 48–20.

The "Alabama Antelope"

Did anyone really know at the time how significant that first play, that first touchdown, would be? On September 22, 1935, when Packers quarterback Arnie Herber hooked up with Don Hutson, a rookie wide receiver from the University of Alabama, pro football was forever changed.

On that early fall afternoon against the Chicago Bears, Hutson demonstrated—with an 83-yard touchdown catch and run—that he was already an integral and indispensable part of the team. At 6'1" and 183 pounds, Hutson had the size and speed to drive rival defenses crazy, and he provided an offensive spark for a team that certainly needed one.

Ironically, Hutson, who went on to become one of the greatest Packers in team history, almost played for another franchise. These were the days before the NFL draft, and amateur players could sign wherever they chose. Hutson signed with both the Packers and the Brooklyn Dodgers. NFL president Joe Carr was called upon to decide the dispute and ruled in favor of the Packers, supposedly because Green Bay's contract had an earlier postmark.

More than six decades after his retirement from football, Don Hutson (on left with Curly Lambeau) still holds several Packers receiving records.

Lambeau rewarded Hutson with the richest contract in team history—$300 per game. And he was worth every penny.

Hutson played for the Packers for 11 seasons and held most of their receiving records for decades. While with the team, he caught 488 passes and 99 touchdowns, the latter of which remains a team record. As the NFL's most outstanding player in 1941 and 1942, he was awarded the Joe F. Carr Trophy (a precursor to the MVP Award). Hutson was inducted into the Pro Football Hall of Fame in 1963 and the Packers Hall of Fame in 1972. He is still considered one of the NFL's greatest receivers.

Don Hutson (right) was nicknamed the "Alabama Antelope" for his speed and agility on the gridiron.

Dynamic Duo

Don Hutson got off to a dramatic start in his first professional game, but he truly blossomed as a great receiver when he paired up with quarterback Cecil Isbell beginning in 1938. Isbell and Hutson hit it off immediately. It didn't hurt that they worked at the same factory during the off-season and practiced pass patterns in the parking lot during their lunch breaks.

From 1940 to 1942, Isbell and Hutson were the NFL's premier aerial show, as Hutson caught 34 touchdown passes— 17 in 1942 alone. But after that season, Isbell quit pro football after playing for just five years. He told friends he wanted to go out on his own terms and not face being cut by Lambeau down the road.

Cecil Isbell (left) and Don Hutson honed their timing by tossing the pigskin outside the factory where they both worked during the off-season.

1936 NFL Champs: Back on Top Again

In the four seasons since the Green Bay Packers had won their last NFL championship, the team—and the league—had transformed. It was now 1936, and almost everything was different.

The Packers had a different personality on the field. Gone were stalwarts such as Verne Lewellen, "Iron Mike" Michalske, Cal Hubbard, and Lavvie Dilweg. They had been replaced by a new set of stars that included receiver Don Hutson, running back Bob Monnett, guard Hank Bruder, and lineman Charles "Buckets" Goldenberg. Also on board was the ubiquitous Johnny (Blood) McNally, who had spent the 1934 season playing for Pittsburgh.

The one constant? Curly Lambeau on the sidelines.

Changes had come to the NFL as well. A college draft was instituted prior to the 1936 season, and the league, which had long been plagued by franchises coming and going, finally saw a season during which no teams were added and, more importantly, none folded. Also, a championship game—which pitted the winners of the NFL's Western and Eastern Divisions in a battle for the league title—had been added in 1933.

As Lambeau examined his roster, he liked what he saw—a promising team with a real chance to win another championship. He hadn't had confidence like that in his players for five years.

After starting the season 1–1 (including a humbling 30–3 home loss to the Bears), the Packers ripped off nine straight wins before ending the season with a scoreless tie against the Chicago Cardinals. The Pack finished the regular season 10–1–1 and slipped past the Bears for the Western Division title when the Bears were upset by their crosstown rival, the Cardinals.

That set up an NFL title game with the Boston Redskins, winners of the Eastern Division and a team that was beset by uncertainty and turmoil. Team owner George Preston Marshall had already decided to move the team to Washington, D.C., because of poor fan support. Then, the Redskins had to give up home-field advantage for the title game (in favor of New York City's Polo Grounds) because of bad field conditions.

In front of nearly 30,000 fans, the Packers jumped on the Redskins early when quarterback Arnie Herber connected with Hutson on a 48-yard touchdown pass. Second-half touchdown runs by Milt Gantenbein and Bob Monnett were all the Packers needed to coast past the Redskins 21–6 to secure their fourth league title.

And when it was over, Lambeau, who didn't dispense praise easily, honored his new champs. "These Packers are as fine a squad of men as ever represented any city," he said. "They have been marvelous, not only on the football field...but in their everyday relations toward their work, their coaches, and the city they represent."

High praise coming from Lambeau. High praise, indeed.

1936 GREEN BAY PACKERS: Back Row: Laws, Herber, Schneidman, Letlow, Becker, Miller, Hinkle, Hutson, Gantenbein, Monnett; Middle Row: Lambeau, Scherer, Bruder, Gordon, Svendsen, Kiesling, Blood, Smith, Johnston, Smith; Front Row: Paulekas, Engebretsen, Evans, Schwammel, Seibold, Butler, Sauer, Clemens, Goldenberg.

The '36 championship team included Packers legends Don Hutson, Johnny (Blood) McNally, Arnie Herber, Clarke Hinkle, Tiny Engebretsen, Milt Gantenbein, and coach Curly Lambeau.

The Packers celebrated their fourth NFL title with a lavish banquet in Green Bay after defeating the Boston Redskins 21–6 at the Polo Grounds.

Falling Short:
The 1938 Championship Game

With memories of the '36 championship still dancing in their heads, the Packers saw no reason why 1937 wouldn't produce the same result. But early injuries, most notably a separated shoulder suffered by quarterback Arnie Herber, quickly derailed those thoughts. The Packers started the season 0–2, then won seven straight before dropping their last two games, which eliminated them from title contention.

The disappointment of 1937 made the '38 season even more intriguing. Lambeau, who was always looking for ways to motivate and improve his team, made an interesting move in the December draft when he selected quarterback Cecil Isbell, who would eventually replace the injured veteran Herber.

The decision seemed to pay off as the Packers posted an 8–3 record and secured at least a tie for the Western Division title. The only variable was the Detroit Lions, who needed to win their final two games to force a playoff with the Packers. The Lions beat the Bears, but they lost to the Eagles in their season finale, which secured the division for Green Bay.

That sent the Packers back to the Polo Grounds to face the powerful New York Giants, who had beaten the Packers 15–3

The Packers squared off against the New York Giants at the Polo Grounds in a battle for the 1938 NFL championship. Here, Clarke Hinkle is stopped just short of the goal line, but he drove in for a touchdown on the next play.

during the regular season. On December 11, 1938, in front of what was then a record crowd of 48,120, the Packers and Giants, two of the premier franchises in the league, waged a terrific battle.

After falling behind 9–0, the Packers rallied with a touchdown run by Clarke Hinkle and a touchdown pass from Herber (now healed from his persistent shoulder woes) to Carl Mulleneaux. Still, the Pack trailed 16–14 at halftime.

A Tiny Engebretsen field goal in the third quarter gave the Packers the lead, but the Giants responded by driving 61 yards and scoring on a Hank Soar touchdown. The game's most enduring image was Hinkle clinging to Soar's leg, trying desperately to bring him to the ground. Instead, Soar dragged Hinkle for a few yards into the end zone.

And that was it. In search of a second NFL championship in three years, the Packers instead suffered a 23–17 loss. It was a feeling none of the players wanted to remember but were unable to forget.

The Packers were hoping to secure their fifth NFL title in the 1938 championship game, but they lost to the Giants 23–17.

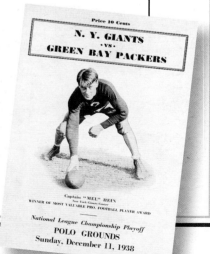

Price 10 Cents

N. Y. GIANTS
-vs.-
GREEN BAY PACKERS

Captain "MEL" HEIN
New York Giants Center
WINNER OF MOST VALUABLE PRO. FOOTBALL PLAYER AWARD

National League Championship Playoff
POLO GROUNDS
Sunday, December 11, 1938

The 1939 Championship: Back for Revenge

Losing can be powerful motivation. And the memory of the 23–17 loss to the New York Giants in the 1938 championship game was never far from the Packers' minds.

The 1939 Green Bay Packers were a formidable team with a number of star players, including Don Hutson, Clarke Hinkle, Tiny Engebretsen, and two quarterbacks who could play for anybody in the league—Arnie Herber and Cecil Isbell. They all did their parts to set up a return date to the championship game by rolling through the season with a 9–2 record, including winning their final four games by a combined score of 70–29.

Arnie Herber was back at the top of his game at quarterback. Star wide receiver Don Hutson, who had battled injuries the previous season, was finally healthy again. And the defense was playing superbly. All the Packers wanted was a rematch with the Giants, who they were convinced they should've beaten the previous season in New York.

The Packers got their wish when the Giants edged the Washington Redskins for the Eastern Division title. This time, though, the game would be played on the Packers' home turf—just not the home everyone expected. In a decision that enraged Green Bay fans, it was decided by the Packers' executive committee that the championship game would be played not at City Stadium in Green Bay but at State Fair Park in Milwaukee.

Rumors of collusion and backroom deals swirled as fans tried to understand why the Green Bay Packers would play for the NFL title 100-plus miles south of Green Bay. Indeed, the final decision wasn't even made until

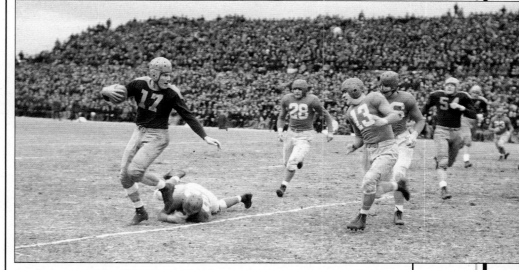

Packers quarterback Cecil Isbell (17) runs for yardage against the New York Giants in the NFL title game held at State Fair Park in Milwaukee on December 10, 1939.

After losing a heartbreaker to the Giants in the '38 playoffs, the Packers got their revenge in '39, coasting to a 27–0 win.

four days before the game, and the Packers announced, rather lamely, that the game was moved to Milwaukee to thank those fans downstate for their years of support. Even now, no one really knows the actual reason for the move, though clearly part of it was the fact that State Fair Park seated more spectators.

And so, on December 10, 1939, more than 32,000 fans showed up on a cold, clear day with winds blowing at more than 35 miles per hour. The result was a dominant Packers performance.

Green Bay intercepted six passes and held the Giants to just 164 total yards. Isbell and Herber each threw touchdown passes, and the Packers posted the first NFL championship game shutout with a resounding 27–0 win.

The team's résumé was starting to grow quite impressive. In the span of 11 years, the Packers had won five NFL titles and probably should have had a sixth. This was a franchise that was at the top of its game, and no one saw any reason for that success to end. Reality, however, had other ideas.

SOUVENIR
Official Program

GREEN BAY PACKERS
NEW YORK GIANTS

SUNDAY
DEC. 10
1939

STATE FAIR PARK MILWAUKEE

PRICE
KICKOFF
1:30 P.M.
25¢

RESERVED
SEC. ROW SEAT
D 33
DEC. 10, 1939
EST. PRICE — $2.00
FED. TAX — .20
TOTAL — $2.20

WORLD'S PROFESSIONAL CHAMPIONSHIP

Game Day

By the end of the 1930s, the Green Bay Packers owned five NFL titles and were one of the most stable and recognizable franchises in the league. But facts were facts. In a league that featured teams in Chicago, New York City, Philadelphia, Cleveland, and Detroit, Green Bay remained a quaint anachronism and, by far, the smallest city with a franchise. Travel to Green Bay was never easy in the best of circumstances, and it was worse when the frigid temps and snowy weather blew in.

And, of course, there were always rumors that the team might up and move someday, though there was never a concrete offer from anywhere else. At the same time, City Stadium, which at one time had been one of the league's top facilities, was starting to fall behind other NFL venues.

City Stadium, seen here in 1938, served the Packers well as their home turf from 1925 to 1956. During that time, the Pack racked up six NFL titles, putting the small city of Green Bay on the map.

Taking to the Skies

Curly Lambeau could see the future, and it was in the clouds.

Until 1940, teams playing on the road literally went on the road, often traveling to games by bus or train. But for the November 17, 1940, game against the Giants in New York, Lambeau chartered two planes. It would be the first time any NFL team flew to a game, and it turned out to be a better idea in theory than in practice.

The Packers traveled to Chicago, where they boarded what was supposed to be a nonstop flight to New York. But the team equipment weighed so much that the planes needed extra fuel and were forced to land in Cleveland to gas up.

While waiting, airline officials learned that dense fog was causing a fearsome air traffic backup in New York. Lambeau was told that there could also be additional fuel issues later on, which might force the planes back to Cleveland. So, in the end, Lambeau put his team on a train for the duration of the trip. The travel-weary Packers ended up losing to the Giants 7–3.

Frequent renovations had increased the facility's seating capacity to 25,000, but visiting teams were still forced to dress in the East High School locker room or, in many cases, in their hotel rooms. It wasn't like that at Chicago's Wrigley Field or the Polo Grounds in New York.

The accommodations were better for the Packers, who had their own locker room, but the grumbling from visiting teams made Packers officials glad they played at least one game per season in Milwaukee. Some teams even lobbied to be the opponent that played in Milwaukee because it afforded the visitors a chance to play in a "big city" atmosphere.

Nevertheless, the spartan conditions at City Stadium clearly worked to the Packers' advantage, and from 1930 to 1939, they rolled up a 50–13–2 record at home. Talk about a home-field advantage.

The 1941 Packers: Good, But Not Quite Good Enough

After their impressive victory over the New York Giants to claim the 1939 NFL title, the Packers seemed to be in the midst of one of those rare, wondrous periods when everything falls into place.

The Packers of this era were loaded with talent—including Cecil Isbell, Don Hutson, and Clarke Hinkle—but, for some reason, the Packers of 1940 were not able to re-create the magic of 1939. They never really found their stride and fell to 6–4–1, the team's poorest record since they went 7–6 in 1934.

And although they clearly struggled all season, the Packers were still in the running for the Western Division title until the final week of the season, when the Chicago Bears beat the Chicago Cardinals to secure the division title.

So as the 1941 season dawned, the Packers knew they had much to prove—again. But the season got off to an uneasy start with the retirement of steady end Milt Gantenbein and contract holdouts by veteran stars Hinkle and Arnie Herber. In the end, both signed, with Hinkle receiving a $10,000 contract, the largest in club history. Herber didn't fare quite as well. After signing, the 11-year veteran was released during the preseason, and one of the first great quarterbacks in team history was gone.

But this remained an impressive squad—one that went on to post a commanding 10–1 record. The team's only loss came at the hands of Sid Luckman and the Chicago Bears on September 28. The Packers returned the favor on November 2 in Chicago with a 16–14 victory.

In 1941, the Packers and the Bears both finished 10–1, with each team's only loss coming at the hands of the other. So on December 14, 1941, the two teams faced off in a playoff game to decide the Western Division title.

It seemed almost inevitable that the two best teams in the Western Division would meet again. And indeed when both teams finished the regular season 10–1, it set up a third meeting—the NFL's first-ever playoff game to determine the division champ.

And so, on December 14, a week after the attack on Pearl Harbor propelled America into World War II, the Packers jumped out to a quick 7–0 lead against the Bears in front of more than 43,000 fans at Wrigley Field. But that's all the Packers would celebrate.

The Bears roared back with 30 unanswered points and racked up 267 rushing yards on their way to a convincing 33–14 win to claim the division title. Chicago went on to beat the New York Giants 37–9 for the NFL crown.

Never before had the Packers posted such a stellar record and not reached a league championship game. Indeed, except for perhaps the 1997 squad, this may have been the best Packers team that did not win a title. It was an opportunity missed, and with America now at war, no one really knew what the future held.

Clarke Hinkle is brought down by two Bears players during a November 3, 1940, contest at Wrigley Field. The Packers lost the game 14–7 and finished the season 6–4–1, but they just missed a trip to the championship game.

CHICAGO BEARS vs. GREEN BAY

OFFICIAL PROGRAM

WRIGLEY FIELD
CHICAGO
BEARS vs. GREEN BAY
PACKERS
Dec. 14
1941
GRAND STAND - 2.50

Dec. 14

M R 2C
R 3
GRAND STAND 2.50
KICK-OFF
1:15 P.M.

SUNDAY SEPT. 28th .... PRICE 10¢

The Packers During War Time

By the time the 1942 NFL season rolled around, nothing was the same. The United States was deeply invested in World War II, and thousands upon thousands of young men were being sent to all parts of the globe.

Not surprisingly, the NFL was dramatically impacted. By the start of the season, roughly a hundred NFL players were serving in the armed forces. The Packers alone lost 15 players from the 1941 team, including star back Clarke Hinkle. Of the 20 players Green Bay selected in the '42 draft, only 18th-round pick Bob Ingalls had the chance to make the team.

In 1943, with player shortages growing, the Cleveland Rams suspended operations for a year. The Philadelphia Eagles and Pittsburgh Steelers merged that season to become a strange amalgamation known as the Phil-Pitt Steagles. It seemed that desperate times called for desperate measures.

But it was also an amazing time. In 1942, with Cecil Isbell at quarterback and Don Hutson at wide receiver, the Packers put on the kind of aerial show never before seen in the NFL. In 11 games, Isbell threw for 2,021 yards and an incredible 24 touchdowns. No Packers quarterback would throw for as many yards during a season until Tobin Rote had 2,311 in 1954, and no quarterback would toss as many TD passes until Lynn Dickey threw 32 in 1983.

On the receiving end of most of those passes was Hutson, who grabbed 74 passes for 1,211 yards and 17 touchdowns. These, too, were records that were built to last. Indeed, it would take until 1952 for Billy Howton to break the yardage mark (1,231), until 1989 for Sterling Sharpe to break the receptions record (90), and until 1994 for Sharpe to break the TD record (18).

By 1944, the Packers were back in a familiar position: playing the New York Giants for the NFL title. But the faces had changed—Irv Comp had taken over at quarterback when Isbell

CHAMPION SERIES

1944 GREEN BAY PACKERS

WORLD CHAMPIONS

Rear Row: Curly Lambeau, Head Coach; Don Hutson; Paul Berezney; Ade Schwammel; Irv Comp; Tiny Croft; Alex Urban; Bob Kahler; Baby Ray; Mike Bucchianneri; George Trafton, Assistant Coach.
Middle Row: Bud Jorgensen, Trainer; Bill Kuusisto; Ray Wehba; Glenn Sorenson; Bob Flowers; Harry Jacunski; Ted Fritsch; Don Perkins; Charles Tollefson; Joel Mason; Gus Seaburg, Assistant Trainer.
Front Row: Charles Goldenberg; Paul Duhart; Ben Starrett; Pete Tinsley; Forrest McPherson; Larry Craig; Charlie Brock; Lou Brock; Roy McKay; Joe Laws.

The 1944 Packers would be the last Green Bay team to finish above third place for more than a decade. Curly Lambeau and his squad bested the New York Giants 14–7 on December 17, 1944, to secure the sixth NFL championship in franchise history.

retired after the 1942 season, and Ted Fritsch was the new running star. Hutson was still around, but football no longer inspired him as it had before. His brother had been killed in the war, and he was looking forward to a career in business after football.

But Hutson's reputation was enough. Using him as a decoy, the 8–2 Packers dominated the Giants on the ground. Fritsch scored two touchdowns, and journeyman Joe Laws ran for 74 yards on offense and intercepted three passes on defense as the Packers won 14–7.

It was Green Bay's sixth NFL title since 1929 and, though no one knew it at the time, it would mark the end of an era.

AAFC vs. the NFL

The NFL had hoped to get back to something resembling normalcy in 1946. The war was over, players were returning, and everything would be as it had been.

Except, of course, it wasn't.

Looming large was a new rival league, the All-American Football Conference (AAFC), which presented a vibrant and impressive challenge to the heretofore domination of the NFL.

The AAFC featured teams in Brooklyn, Buffalo, Chicago, Cleveland, Miami, and New York, and also did something that really caught the NFL's attention—it located franchises on the fertile and profitable West Coast, sprouting teams in Los Angeles and San Francisco.

The AAFC signed a number of high-profile players, including Heisman Trophy winners Frank Sinkwich and Angelo Bertelli, as well as more than a hundred players with NFL experience.

The Packers were unscathed by the AAFC pillaging, but they had their own set of problems, including the retirement of the irreplaceable Don Hutson after the 1945 season. His loss was felt immediately as the Packers' air attack came to a virtual standstill.

After Hutson had led the Packers in receiving for ten seasons, the Packers' top receivers in '46 were Clyde Goodnight and Nolan Luhn, with 16 receptions each. In comparison, Hutson's

In 1946, Clyde Goodnight (above) and Nolan Luhn tied for the team lead with 16 receptions each. However, Goodnight ran for more yards, 308 compared to Luhn's 224.

worst season with the Packers was 1935—his rookie season—and he still caught 18 passes that year.

As for the AAFC, it put up a good fight, but after the 1949 season, it reached an agreement with the NFL. Three teams—the Cleveland Browns, Baltimore Colts, and San Francisco 49ers—merged into the NFL, and the AAFC folded.

Getting Up to Speed

Curly Lambeau always seemed to be ahead of the curve, whether it was his belief in the forward pass or his ability to find the right player for the right situation.

But by 1947, the Packers were behind the times, and it was beginning to show on the field. Most teams in the NFL had embraced the new T-formation—a running attack that relied on speed and misdirection. The Bears and Giants had perfected it but the Packers had stayed with the single wing—a blunt, straight-ahead style of offense that no longer seemed to fit with the new NFL. In the T-formation, the quarterback was under center rather than taking the snap in the backfield. When offenses ran plays from the T, defenders had to wait to see who had the ball, which meant more fakes, more deception, and more chances for big plays.

Curly Lambeau (right) outlines a play for Don Hutson (left) and Cecil Isbell in 1940. The Packers switched to the T-formation seven years later.

The Pack adopted the T-formation in 1947, and by 1949, they had the hang of it. That year, Tony Canadeo rushed for 1,052 yards, setting a team record that stood until 1960, when Jim Taylor rushed for 1,101 yards.

Packers wide receiver Don Hutson won the Joe F. Carr trophy for league MVP in both 1941 and 1942.

By 1944, the Packers had nailed down six NFL titles, so Packer Backers of this era proudly displayed pennants such as the one shown here.

One of the Packers' true all-time legends, Don Hutson had his No. 14 jersey retired in 1951. He was the first Packer to have his number retired.

This advertisement from the late 1930s showcases some of the Packers' star players of the time, including Don Hutson, Arnie Herber, and Clarke Hinkle.

This football from the 1930s represents the type of ball used by players of the era.

"Buckets" Goldenberg (43) got his nickname from a high school coach, who told him to keep his "bucket" (i.e., his rear end) down while in his three-point stance.

This team photo is autographed by the 1936 NFL champion Green Bay Packers.

NATIONAL LEAGUE FOOTBALL

CHICAGO CARDS VS. GREEN BAY PACKERS

CITY STADIUM
GREEN BAY
SUNDAY **OCT. 11**

Ernie Nevers and his Cardinals have always given the Packers lots of trouble. Last year, they broke the Bay's winning streak in Chicago, all the Cards' stars of 1930 are back in togs and the recruits have shown class in the early games.

SEE Nevers, Slater, Blumer, Erickson, Kassel, Hill, Holmer and Glassgow. These are the gridders who win football games for the Cards.

3000 Additional Seats Have Been Erected
Every Seat in Park Reserved

Kickoff 2 o'clock   Admission Prices: $1, 1.25, 1.50, $2   — Buy Your Tickets Early and Be Sure of a Seat

From 1934 to 1969, the Ed Thorp Memorial Trophy was awarded to the NFL champion. The Packers received these in 1939 (left) and 1936.

In the 1920s and '30s, football players wore leather shoulder pads like these, which belonged to legendary Packers halfback Johnny (Blood) McNally.

This poster was used to promote a 1931 game against the Chicago Cardinals at City Stadium. The Pack prevailed 26-7.

Stars of the Era

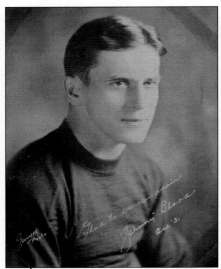

Above: *The "Vagabond Half-back," Johnny McNally was a colorful character and a free spirit.* Below: *After football, Cal Hubbard had a second career as an MLB umpire.*

A s a highly gifted student, **Johnny (Blood) McNally** graduated from high school at age 14. In college, he was equally as talented on the athletic field. He played in the NFL for 14 years with five different teams; he spent seven of those seasons in Green Bay. After joining the Packers in 1929, McNally led the team to three straight NFL titles. His mark of 230 career points is still among the top 25 in team history.

After football, McNally returned to college, earned a degree in economics, and even wrote a textbook on the subject. He was inducted into the Pro Football Hall of Fame in 1963 and the Packers Hall of Fame in 1970.

One of the NFL's great early defensive linemen, **Robert "Cal" Hubbard** started with the New York Giants in 1927 but joined the Packers in 1929 and played with them until 1933 and again in 1935. He was an All-Pro from 1931 to 1933. Although he was 6'5" and 250 pounds, Hubbard was often faster than the running backs he tackled. He later became a Major League umpire and is the only person in the Baseball

(1976), College Football (1962), and Pro Football (1963) Halls of Fame. He is also in the Packers Hall of Fame (1970).

Although **Clarke Hinkle** never gained more than 552 yards in a season, his mark of 3,860 career yards (1932–41) still ranks in the Packers' all-time top ten. In 1937, Hinkle scored a touchdown in six straight games and rushed for 552 yards in 11 games. In 1938, he led the league in scoring with 58 points (seven touchdowns, three field goals, and seven PATs), and he led the NFL in field goals in 1940 and '41. He finished his career with 44 touchdowns.

Hinkle was also a linebacker, and, according to some teammates, perhaps the hardest hitter on the team. He was inducted into the Pro Football Hall of Fame in 1964 and the Packers Hall of Fame in 1972, and was named to the NFL's All-Time Two-Way Team in 1994. In 1997, the Packers' practice field on Oneida Street, across from Lambeau Field, was named in his honor.

August "Iron Mike" Michalske played three seasons with football's New York Yankees before joining the Packers in 1929 and playing in Green Bay through 1935 and again in 1937. Michalske played both offense and defense and was known as one of the toughest linemen in football. This toughness, coupled with his ability to play 60 minutes every game and the fact that he was never injured, earned him

Above: *Clarke Hinkle was a fullback, linebacker, place-kicker, and punter.* Below: *"Iron Mike" Michalske wore nine uniform numbers in as many years with the Packers—a team record.*

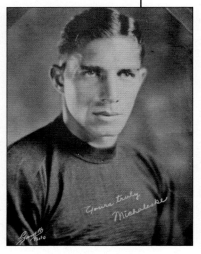

Above: *As a teen, Arnie Herber sold programs at Packers games and dreamed of playing for the team.*
Below: *After football, "Buckets" Goldenberg had a successful restaurant in Milwaukee and was a longtime member of the Packers' board of directors.*

his memorable nickname. He was elected to the Pro Football Hall of Fame in 1964, the first guard ever so honored, and was a charter member of the Packers Hall of Fame in 1970.

Green Bay native **Arnie Herber** idolized the Pack growing up. While working as a handyman for the team, he impressed Curly Lambeau in a tryout. Herber made the team and went on to play 11 seasons for the Packers (1930–40). He was an All-Pro in 1932 and won three NFL passing titles (1932, '34, '36). His mark of 66 touchdown passes still ranks among the top ten in team history.

Herber was inducted into the Pro Football Hall of Fame in 1966 and the Packers Hall of Fame in 1972.

Born in Russia in 1911, **Charles "Buckets" Goldenberg** and his family emigrated to Milwaukee when he was four. He was a star player in high school and an All-Big Ten back and tackle on offense and linebacker on defense at the University of Wisconsin.

Originally a quarterback, Goldenberg was later moved to offensive guard, where he became an All-Pro

player. He played for the Packers from 1933 to 1945, served on the team's board of directors from 1953 to 1985, and was inducted into the Packers Hall of Fame in 1972.

Known as the "Gray Ghost of Gonzaga" thanks to his prematurely gray hair, **Tony Canadeo** was an underrated ninth-round draft choice picked up by the Packers in 1941; he went on to become one of the best and most versatile players in team history. Indeed, he rushed for 4,197 yards, caught 69 passes, threw for 1,642 yards and 16 touchdowns, returned punts and kickoffs, and even finished with nine interceptions from his

Tony Canadeo did it all on the gridiron. Playing both offense and defense, he was perhaps the most versatile and best all-around player in Packers' history.

defensive back position. He was also the first 1,000-yard rusher in team history. His No. 3 was retired in 1952; it was just the second number in team history to be honored in such a way. He was inducted into both the Packers Hall of Fame and the Pro Football Hall of Fame in 1974.

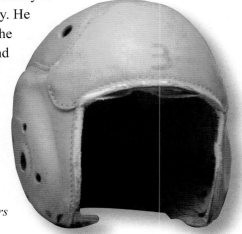

Although Tony Canadeo's No. 3 was retired in 1952, it was accidentally assigned to kicker Ben Agajanian, who played three games for the Packers in 1961.

Packers Upheaval

Everything was about to change in the world of the Green Bay Packers. It was the end of the 1940s, and although no one really knew it at the time, the warning signs were already present.

After the Packers beat the New York Giants for the 1944 NFL championship, the team almost immediately began to slip. They fell to 6–4 in 1945, and then to 6–5 in 1946, finishing third in the Western Division both times. The Packers hadn't finished that low in the division since 1934.

Moreover, Curly Lambeau, the cofounder, architect, and soul of the franchise, was changing, too. He had remarried after a turbulent divorce and was spending more time in California with his new wife than he was in Green Bay. His once idyllic relationships with the executive committee and members of the "Hungry Five" were starting to deteriorate in a wave of accusations about overspending, ego, and lack of production on the field.

These events escalated after the 1946 season, when Lambeau convinced the executive committee to shell out $25,000 to purchase what he envisioned as a state-of-the-art training facility—Rockwood Lodge.

Located 17 miles northeast of town on a bluff overlooking the bay, Lambeau saw Rockwood Lodge as a place where the players could train away from the fans and annoyances of Green Bay.

The 1949 Green Bay Packers pose in front of Rockwood Lodge, which served as their training facility from 1946 to 1949. Rockwood Lodge is believed to have been the first self-contained training camp in NFL history.

Team officials thought it was Lambeau's way of getting away from the people who were trying to tell him what to do. It also upset Packers fans, who felt that the team was no longer accessible to them.

Another shock came in March 1947. George Calhoun, who had helped found the team with Lambeau in 1919 and had been the team's public relations director, was unexpectedly fired by Lambeau. What's more, Lambeau did not even have the dignity to inform his longtime partner of his ouster in person. Instead, Calhoun found out that he'd been sacked while reading wire service reports at the *Press-Gazette*.

Lambeau also dismissed "Hungry Five" member Dr. W. Webber Kelly as team doctor. Four months later, another original "Hungry Five" member, Lee Joannes, resigned and was replaced by Emil Fischer, who was no fan of Lambeau's. It was all coming apart, both on and off the field.

The executive committee moved to limit Lambeau's power by hiring more members and by forcing Lambeau to consult with the body on just about every decision. Those events, plus the Rockwood Lodge fiasco and the fact that the Packers were struggling on the field, led many to conclude that something had to be done—and soon.

Lambeau's Farewell

The Curly Lambeau era ended the way most tenures of this caliber tend to—with questions, confusion, anger, and, yes, a dreadful feeling that something important was gone and would never be found again.

The Packers continued to sink in the Western Division, falling to 3–9 in 1948 and 2–10 in 1949, the worst season in team history to that point. So after the first game of the '49 season, a 17–0 home loss to the Bears, Curly Lambeau handed head-coaching duties to three of his assistants—Tom Stidham, Charley Brock, and Bob Snyder—so he could concentrate on his duties as general manager. But things still did not improve on the playing field.

Then came the confluence of events that changed the Packers for good. Lambeau's contract was scheduled to expire after the '49 season, but in November of that year, the board of directors had voted, after a heated discussion, to extend his contract by two years.

In this 1949 photo, Curly Lambeau walks out of Rockwood Lodge. A few months later, he would walk away from the Packers after 30 years.

But by late January 1950, Lambeau had not signed the contract. At around that same time, in the kind of irony you can't invent, the controversial Rockwood Lodge, which still served as the Packers' training facility, burned to the ground as a result of faulty wiring.

It seemed to symbolize the relationship between the Packers and Lambeau at that stage. And so, on January 30, 1950, citing "dangerous disunity of purpose within the corporation," Lambeau resigned and accepted the post of vice president and head coach of the Chicago Cardinals.

Lambeau had helped to create the Green Bay Packers in 1919 with little more than an idea and a belief that Green Bay could be a great football town. In 30 years, he had produced six league championships and, eventually, seven Pro Football Hall of Famers. But it was over, and someone had to pick up the pieces.

Coming to the Rescue

In 1949, the Packers were struggling on the field, there was volatility in the front office, and the rival All-American Football Conference was considering merging with the NFL.

And although attendance at Packers games remained strong, the team was $90,000 in debt by November 1949, and that didn't help ease concerns among many that the team could be sold, folded, or merged into the new-look league that was coming.

True to form, the Packers put out an SOS to the community, and on Thanksgiving Day, the organization held an intrasquad game in the hopes that it would raise enough money to keep the team alive.

A number of former Packers—including Don Hutson, Lavvie Dilweg, Arnie Herber, and Johnny McNally—were invited to participate. Although it was played in a blizzard at City Stadium, the game drew 12,000 fans and raised $50,000, which allowed the team to avert yet another financial disaster.

PACKERS PARAPHERNALIA

OFFICIAL PROGRAM

CLEVELAND
VS.
GREEN BAY

SUNDAY,
OCT. 22D

PRICE 10¢

When Cleveland Rams offensive lineman Albie Reisz stepped out of the end zone with the ball during this 1944 matchup, it gave the Packers a two-point safety to put the game out of reach. Green Bay won 30–21.

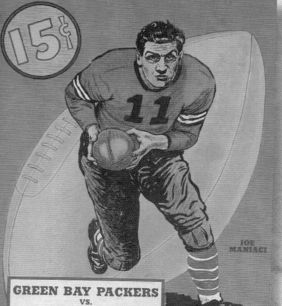

15¢

11

JOE MANIACI

GREEN BAY PACKERS
VS.
CHICAGO BEARS
Sunday, November 5, 1939
WRIGLEY FIELD · CHICAGO

In this 1939 game, the Packers racked up 356 offensive yards to the Bears' 303, but it was not enough. In one of only two losses that season, the Pack went down 30–27. But Green Bay got the last laugh—they went on to win their fifth NFL title later that season.

The Packers scored 21 points in the first quarter, and that was all they really needed to soar past the Eagles 27–20 when the two teams met on September 15, 1940.

OFFICIAL PROGRAM
Philadelphia Eagles
SUNDAY, SEPTEMBER 15, 1940—2 P.M.

PRICE 10¢

On September 24, 1944, the Bears briefly tied the game in the fourth quarter, but the Pack responded with two more touchdowns to put it away by a final score of 42–28.

OFFICIAL PROGRAM

	1	2	3	4	TOTAL
CHICAGO BEARS	0	7	14	7	28
VS. GREEN BAY	14	14	0	14	42

PRICE 10 CENTS

SUNDAY, SEPT. 24th

Fullback Eddie Jankowski played five seasons with the Packers. His 1941 contract shows that he received $200 per game, with incentives for a $250 bonus if he had a good year. However, 1941 was Jankowski's worst year in the NFL, and he retired at the end of the season.

Packers players wore wool sweaters (right) or side-line capes like the one above to keep warm during the 1930s and '40s, when the official team colors were still blue and gold.

The 1939 Green Bay Packers finished the regular season with four straight wins before knocking off the New York Giants 27–0 for the NFL championship.

CHAPTER THREE

THE GOLDEN AGE
1950–1967

"We're not just going to start with a new slate, we're going to throw the old slate away."

VINCE LOMBARDI

Above: *With five NFL titles (including two Super Bowl victories) in the 1960s, the Green Bay Packers were indeed on top of the world.* **Right:** *Coach Vince Lombardi is carried off the field after the Packers beat the Dallas Cowboys 34–27 to win the NFL championship on January 1, 1967. The victory gave Green Bay a chance to face the AFL champion Kansas City Chiefs in the first-ever Super Bowl.*

Changing of the Guard

Now what? With Curly Lambeau gone, the Packers knew they needed to act quickly and decisively to find a replacement. Five days after Lambeau resigned, the Packers' executive board hired Gene Ronzani, an assistant coach for the Chicago Bears, to assume the unenviable task of replacing Lambeau.

Ronzani wasn't the first coach—nor would he be the last—to learn just how difficult it is to replace a legend. But in his favor, Ronzani had strong Wisconsin ties. He grew up in Iron Mountain, which is located in Michigan's Upper Peninsula, a mere two hours from Green Bay. He was also a star football player at Milwaukee's Marquette University before joining the Bears, first as a player, then as a coach. But unfortunately for Ronzani, Lambeau had left very little in the cupboard for him to work with.

Gene Ronzani (above) replaced legendary Packers coach Curly Lambeau in 1950, but he resigned with two games left to play in the '53 season.

It showed in the 1950 opener, when the Packers were crushed at home by the Detroit Lions 45–7. Though Green Bay won its next two games, the spiral that had begun two years earlier continued, as the Packers finished 3–9. They posted an identical record in 1951, and although the Packers improved to 6–6 in 1952, they ended that season with a three-game losing streak. After starting the 1953 season 2–7–1, Ronzani resigned with two games remaining, and assistant coaches Hugh Devore and Ray "Scooter" McLean took over.

But if there was a silver lining to the Ronzani era, it was that, once again, Packers fans came to the rescue financially. It had already been decided that the Packers would hold another stock sale in November 1949 to help raise money. The stock sold at $25 a share, and fans bought $118,000 worth.

They had saved the team again, but was this a team worth saving?

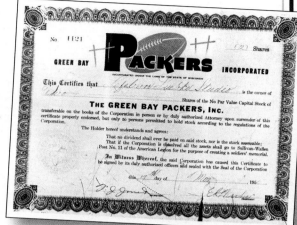

In 1950, the Packers held another stock sale to raise much-needed cash for the team. Shares sold for $25 apiece; the holder of this stock certificate purchased two shares.

Division of Labor

With the All-American Football Conference (AAFC) folding and three of its teams merging into the NFL, the March 1950 league meeting saw several changes weaved into the very fabric of the league. Most notably, the NFL was split into the American and National conferences beginning in the 1950 season.

The Packers took their place in the National Conference along with the Bears, Lions, Los Angeles Rams, and New York Yanks, as well as the San Francisco 49ers and Baltimore Colts from the AAFC.

The American Conference featured the Chicago Cardinals, New York Giants, Philadelphia Eagles, Pittsburgh Steelers, and Washington Redskins, along with the Cleveland Browns from the AAFC.

The NFL of present day had begun to take shape.

A Mann Among Men

Though Gene Ronzani's career in Green Bay wasn't marked with much success on the field, he was responsible for two major events in franchise history. First, in the 1950 season opener, he unveiled—on a permanent basis—the green and gold color scheme that would become the team's trademark. Second, and more important, he signed Bob Mann, the Packers' first African American player, that same year.

Quiet and unassuming, Mann wanted nothing more than to play football. He didn't care to be a lightning rod for civil rights or seek to break any color barriers. But he also knew that he couldn't avoid what was to come, and he handled it all with dignity and grace.

Mann was an honorable mention All-American receiver at the University of Michigan before signing with the Detroit Lions in 1948, where he and Melvin Groomes became the Lions' first black players.

In 1949, his second season, Mann caught 66 passes for a league-best 1,014 yards, but in 1950, he was traded by the Lions to the New York Yanks for quarterback Bobby Layne. The Yanks released him soon after, and he was picked up by the Packers.

At 5'11" and 175 pounds, Mann was considered small, even by the NFL standards of the day. But in 1951, he was the Packers' leading receiver, catching 50 passes for 696 yards and eight touchdowns. And while Mann always maintained that his skin color never caused any problems with teammates during his days with the Packers, he did face his share of issues when the team went on the road.

Bob Mann was the Packers' first African American player. He was a member of the Green and Gold from 1950 to 1954.

After all, this was the 1950s, and racial segregation was still in full effect in many regions of the country. Mann often had to stay at a different hotel from his white teammates. Former *Press-Gazette* sportswriter Art Daley recalled an incident in Baltimore: Following a team meeting, Mann headed to his hotel accompanied by white teammate Dick Afflis. After hailing a cab, the two men were told that Mann could not ride in the taxi because he was black. Afflis, a 252-pounder, allegedly grabbed the cabbie by the shirt and politely said, "You take him where he wants to go." He did.

Mann's career was cut short by a knee injury, and he was released by the Packers midway through the 1954 season. He finished his career in Green Bay with 109 receptions and 17 touchdowns, and in 1988, he was inducted into the Packers Hall of Fame.

After retiring from football, Mann went to law school and worked as an attorney in Detroit for 30 years. He died in 2006 at age 82.

Bob Mann and other black players in the NFL in the 1950s paved the way for future African American football players, such as Jim Brown, Reggie White, Emmitt Smith, and Barry Sanders.

Giving Thanks

Thanksgiving and football have gone together for as long as there has been, well, Thanksgiving and football. But the event that has become a holiday tradition really got its start in 1951, when the Detroit Lions routed the visiting Green Bay Packers 52–35 in what is still the highest-scoring Thanksgiving Day game. And every Thanksgiving from 1951 to 1963, the Packers traveled to Detroit's Tiger Stadium, typically to gain little more than a case of heartburn.

During this era, the Packers were truly struggling on the field, while the Lions were enjoying the only real extended success in the franchise's history. In fact, the Lions won three NFL titles during that span—1952, 1953, and 1957—while Green Bay was suffering through a period of mediocrity. The result of this inequity was that from 1951 to 1963, the Packers were just 3–9–1 when the two teams faced each other on Thanksgiving, including losses in the first five contests.

There was just something about the short week of preparation that bothered the Packers in ways that didn't affect the Lions. True, it was always a home game for Detroit because the league awarded the Lions perpetual rights to the Thanksgiving Day game, but the travel to Detroit from Green Bay wasn't exactly a grueling endeavor. Still, the Packers never really looked forward to the trip, and even when Green Bay returned to prominence under Vince Lombardi in the 1960s, the Thanksgiving Day game was no easy task.

For evidence of this, look no further than 1962, a year in which Green Bay went 13–1 and won the NFL championship. The Packers' only loss that season? A 26–14 setback to Detroit on Thanksgiving Day.

The annual series ended after the '63 season—the final game ended in a 13–13 tie—and the two teams did not meet again on the fourth Thursday in November until 1984. Since then, they have faced each other on Thanksgiving Day four more times, including three times in the 21st century.

Packers–Lions Thanksgiving Day Results

November 22, 1951: Lions 52, Packers 35
November 27, 1952: Lions 48, Packers 24
November 26, 1953: Lions 34, Packers 15
November 25, 1954: Lions 28, Packers 24
November 24, 1955: Lions 24, Packers 10
November 22, 1956: Packers 24, Lions 20
November 28, 1957: Lions 18, Packers 6
November 27, 1958: Lions 24, Packers 14
November 26, 1959: Packers 24, Lions 17
November 24, 1960: Lions 23, Packers 10
November 23, 1961: Packers 17, Lions 9
November 22, 1962: Lions 26, Packers 14
November 28, 1963: Packers 13, Lions 13
November 22, 1984: Lions 31, Packers 28
November 27, 1986: Packers 44, Lions 40
November 22, 2001: Packers 29, Lions 27
November 27, 2003: Lions 22, Packers 14
November 22, 2007: Packers 37, Lions 26

From 1951 to 1963, the Packers traveled to Detroit to face the Lions on Thanksgiving Day. More often than not, the Lions feasted on the Green and Gold.

Building a Powerhouse

By the start of the 1952 season, the Green Bay Packers and their weary fans could barely remember the days when the team stood atop the NFL mountain. Since winning their last championship in 1944, it had been a steady journey downhill for the Packers.

Curly Lambeau, the team's original mastermind, was long gone. George Calhoun, cofounder of the franchise, had suffered a bitter separation from the team. The ubiquitous "Hungry Five," who had saved the franchise numerous times with their ability to generate cash, had dispersed. And the team's performance on the field? Oh my! The Packers hadn't tasted a title since 1944, and hadn't even seen the sunny side of the .500 mark since 1947.

Lambeau resigned after the 1949 season, and his replacement, Gene Ronzani, led the Packers to pitiful, back-to-back 3–9 seasons in 1950 and 1951. It seemed that no improvement was in sight. But there was a glimmer of hope for the beleaguered franchise, and it came in the form of the 1952 draft.

In what is generally considered one of the best drafts in team history, the Packers found a number of starters, five of whom would eventually become Pro Bowlers. It started in the first round when Ronzani selected Vito "Babe" Parilli, a quarterback from Kentucky, who immediately replaced veteran Tobin Rote.

In the second round, Green Bay chose Rice wide receiver Billy Howton, who would go on to lead the Packers in receptions for the next six seasons. Bobby Dillon, a defensive back from Texas, was taken in the third round. He still holds the Packers' team record with 52 interceptions in eight seasons.

Dave Hanner, a fifth-round selection from Arkansas, played 13 seasons for the Packers and was a two-time Pro Bowler at defensive tackle. Deral Teteak was a ninth-round pick from Wisconsin who played guard for five seasons and was selected as a Pro Bowler in 1952.

With all this young talent, the Packers made a resurgence in 1952. After losing to the Bears in the season opener, the Packers rebounded to beat an old friend, Curly Lambeau, who by then was coaching the Washington Redskins.

Later that season, the Packers beat the Philadelphia Eagles 12–10 before 10,149 fans at Milwaukee's Marquette Stadium. That was Green Bay's last game at the old park, as Milwaukee County Stadium was set to open the following year.

The Packers were indeed better in 1952, but they still only managed a 6–6 record—their best season since 1947. But it was only a brief respite. The tough times weren't over yet. In fact, they were coming back with a vengeance.

In the 1952 draft, the Packers chose (from left to right) Billy Howton, Vito "Babe" Parilli, Dave Hanner, Bobby Dillon, and Deral Teteak.

The Voice of the Packers

Lee Remmel, the Packers' longtime director of public relations, described Ray Scott's voice better than anyone else: "Everything he said sounded like it was chiseled in stone."

Long before the days of ESPN, sports talk radio, and boisterous announcers, there was Ray Scott. Small of stature and balding, he looked more like a CPA than one of the best radio/TV announcers in football. But that's what he was for more than two decades.

He broadcast just about everything and everywhere, including The Masters, British Open, and U.S. Open golf tournaments; University of Pittsburgh and Drake University sports; and Milwaukee Brewers, Washington Senators, and Minnesota Twins baseball games. And he called nearly every college bowl game at one time or another.

Yet, he is still more closely identified with the Packers than any other team he covered in his 40-plus years in the business. He handled the Packers' play-by-play duties from 1956 through 1967, which corresponded almost perfectly with the Packers' rebirth and domination under Vince Lombardi. Indeed, Scott was part of the Packers' restricted inner circle and would often be invited to Lombardi's house after games.

For fans of a certain age, Scott's smooth tone and economy of words remain the gold standard of sportscasting. His style was simple, direct, and accurate.

"Starr … Dowler … touchdown," he'd say.

"Taylor up the middle … first down," he'd intone.

In his view, that was all that needed to be said. And his style rubbed off on his protégé, a color analyst named Pat Summerall, who had played professionally for the New York Giants. When Scott moved on, Summerall took his place as the game's top NFL announcer, but he always credited Scott for making him the play-by-play man he was.

Scott was in the booth for all of the Packers' great games of the era. He announced the Ice Bowl in 1967. He broadcast the first two Super Bowls, both of which the Packers won. He also called Super Bowls VI and VII for CBS. In his later years, Scott made numerous guest-broadcasting appearances, and, every time, he made it sound like whatever he was calling was the most important event in the nation. In 1993, he closed out his professional career by hosting a sports talk show in Green Bay.

In 1998, Ray Scott died in Minneapolis at age 78. In 2000, the Pro Football Hall of Fame honored him posthumously with the Pete Rozelle Radio-Television Award. He was inducted into the Packers Hall of Fame in 2001.

Longtime Packers announcer Ray Scott introduces the Green Bay Packers. From left to right: Max McGee (85), Fuzzy Thurston (63), Jim Ringo (51), and Jerry Kramer (64).

The Packers Hit Rock Bottom

Two things were crystal clear midway through the Packers' interminable 1953 season: The team was going nowhere fast, and head coach Gene Ronzani had what could charitably be called limited job security.

Ronzani came to the Packers from the Chicago Bears with an impressive résumé as an offensive mastermind. But in three-plus seasons, little of that success had transferred to Green Bay. From 1950 to 1952, he was 12–24, and the '53 campaign was quickly spinning out of control as the Packers lost nine of 12 games (though they did forge a 21–21 tie with the Bears).

But after a listless 34–15 loss to the Detroit Lions on Thanksgiving Day, the executive committee had seen enough and asked for Ronzani's resignation. Assistant coaches Hugh Devore and Ray "Scooter" McLean took over head-coaching duties for the remainder of the season, and the committee went back to the drawing board to find a new coach.

But this time, the executive committee decided, for the first time in club history, to hire a separate general manager to handle the personnel issues that seemed to overwhelm Ronzani (who had been both GM and head coach). To fill these vacancies, the Packers looked to Green Bay's glorious past and hired former star running back Verne Lewellen as general manager and Lisle Blackbourn as the new head coach starting in 1954.

Blackbourn had no pro football experience—neither as a player nor as a coach—but he had built a strong program at Marquette University and was considered a good judge of football talent, as would later become evident.

A Packers first-round draft pick in 1957, Ron Kramer was one of the greatest tight ends in team history. He played seven seasons for Green Bay.

But nothing changed on the field. In his four seasons as head coach, Blackbourn's best record was 6–6 in 1955. And after a 4–8 mark in 1956 and a 3–9 campaign in 1957, the executive committee had again seen enough. Even though Blackbourn had a year left on his contract, the committee fired him in January 1958 and immediately replaced him with popular longtime Packers assistant Ray McLean.

The irony was that, despite his struggles in the standings, Blackbourn was astute enough in the draft room to assemble the pieces that would turn the franchise around and indirectly change the course of NFL history.

Consider this: In the 1956 draft, the Packers selected linemen Forrest Gregg and Bob Skoronski and an unheralded quarterback from Alabama named Bart Starr. In 1957, they took Heisman Trophy-winning quarterback Paul Hornung and tight end Ron Kramer. On December 2, 1957, when the first four rounds of the 1958 NFL draft were held, Blackbourn had a hand in the selections of linebacker Dan Currie, fullback Jim Taylor, linebacker Ray Nitschke, and guard Jerry Kramer. By the time the draft was completed on January 29, 1958, Blackbourn had been fired, so scouting director Jim Vainisi is generally credited with formulating that impressive draft.

Still, Blackbourn's imprint on the future of the franchise had been made.

Above: *Ray McLean only lasted a season as Packers head coach.* **Below:** *Lisle Blackbourn was better in the draft room than he was on the sidelines for the Packers.*

The Pack Gets a New Home

The 1950s had not been kind to the once-proud franchise known as the Green Bay Packers. It started with the resignation of founder Curly Lambeau and continued with poor draft choices and personnel decisions, as well as a procession of coaches who tried hard but couldn't quite get the job done. Disappointment evolved into the realization around Green Bay (and certainly around the league) that the Packers had collapsed into perhaps the worst franchise in all of football. It led to the famous line that has been uttered countless times by as many players who knew that if they didn't do their job on their current team, they could be traded to Green Bay—the NFL's Siberia—and no one wanted that.

The Packers also faced major issues with their stadium. City Stadium had once been the cathedral of the fledgling NFL, but that was in the 1930s. Time and economics had progressed, and the old park was no longer good enough to sustain an NFL team.

In 1956, on the heels of an improved season that saw the Pack go 6–6, the executive committee made the pitch that has been heard in nearly every city with a pro franchise: The board told Green Bay residents that without a new stadium, the NFL was going to move the Packers somewhere else.

It might have been an idle threat, but no one wanted to take the risk. So on April 3, 1956, Green Bay residents voted to pass a bond issue referendum to pay for a new $960,000 stadium that would seat 32,150 fans. It would sit at the corner of Oneida Street and Highland Avenue, and it would be known, once again, as City Stadium.

The new City Stadium was built quickly and was ready to be christened for the start of the 1957 season. And what a day it was! On September 29, the Packers opened their new playground against the only team with whom it made sense to open a new stadium—their archrival, the Chicago Bears.

On hand were dignitaries such as Vice President Richard Nixon and actor James Arness, the star of *Gunsmoke,* the most

On September 29, 1957, the Packers christened their new home, City Stadium—now known as Lambeau Field—by topping the Bears 21–17 in front of 32,132 fans.

popular TV show of the day. There was excitement and fireworks and new optimism for a franchise that hadn't had much to celebrate in several years. And to cap off this perfect day, the Packers beat the Bears 21–17.

But that optimism quickly faded. The Packers lost nine of their next 11 games, and when they played their last home game of the season on November 17, fewer than 20,000 fans were on hand to watch them lose a heartbreaker to the Los Angeles Rams 31–27.

When the new City Stadium opened its doors in 1957, it held 32,150 people. Over the years, capacity has more than doubled, and it presently seats 72,000-plus.

But something special was born that inaugural September afternoon. City Stadium, which would later be renamed Lambeau Field, has since taken its place among the top sports venues in America. It is the longest-serving stadium in the NFL, and it shows no signs of its age. It has undergone seven renovations since it was first built, the most recent was a $295 million redevelopment (2000–2003) that turned it into a full-service family destination that houses restaurants, the Packers Pro Shop, and the Packers Hall of Fame. Gone are the days when the stadium seated barely 32,000 fans; the new Lambeau Field holds more than 70,000.

A Final Farewell to Curly Lambeau

It was time to put the past to rest when the Packers learned on June 1, 1965, that Curly Lambeau had died at age 67. Lambeau did not leave Green Bay on the best of terms. Frustrated by the control exerted by the Packers' executive committee and unhappy about where the franchise was going, Lambeau resigned after the 1949 season to take over the Chicago Cardinals and, eventually, the Washington Redskins.

Lambeau knew, as did the Packers, that the franchise hadn't been the same since he'd left. But the Packers also knew that, despite any ill will that existed toward Lambeau, the man had been the architect and soul of the franchise. And so, as perhaps the ultimate tribute, the organization renamed City Stadium Lambeau Field.

While Vince Lombardi publicly praised the move, inside he was furious. He didn't approve of Lambeau's reputation as a womanizer, and he didn't like the fact that the focus was diverted away from him and his team. But no one can argue that, even today, few stadiums in America are more recognizable than Lambeau Field.

Former team president Bob Harlan often talked about watching the stadium parking lot from the window of his office on any random day and seeing cars pull up. "People will get out, have their picture taken in front of the stadium, and drive away," he said. "It's just something about the place."

Despite the team's woeful records in the 1950s, Green Bay fans never stopped waving Packers pennants.

The Coach: Vince Lombardi

With Vince Lombardi, fact and myth are often intertwined. He was either a madman or a genius, a motivator or a tyrant. He got the best out of his players either because they loved him or because they feared him.

Whatever the truth—and that takes many forms, too—the impact of Lombardi on the Packers and the NFL reverberates even today. This much is certain: The Packers needed somebody like Lombardi just as badly as Lombardi needed a team like the Packers.

Quarterback Bart Starr still remembers the first time he saw Lombardi. It was a preseason game in 1958. Starr was running off the field and saw Lombardi, the offensive coordinator for the New York Giants, yelling not at his offense but at the Giants' defense.

"That showed me his aggressiveness and intensity," Starr later recalled.

And while the Packers and Vince Lombardi will be forever tied together in football history, Lombardi didn't just arrive in Green Bay as a savior. After a horrific 1–10–1 season under Ray McLean in 1958, the Packers were looking to make another major change and were eyeing University of Iowa coach Forest Evashevski as a possible successor.

But the name Vince Lombardi kept popping up. At age 45, Lombardi had never been a head coach of anything beyond the high school ranks, but he was highly regarded around the NFL

NFL royalty: Packers coach Vince Lombardi (left) and Chicago Bears coach George Halas greet each other before a 1961 game at Wrigley Field. They were never close friends, but the men respected each other immensely.

and had impressed Packers president Dominic Olejniczak.

He even got the stamp of approval from George Halas, the coach of the Packers' ancient rival, the Bears. "He's a good one," Halas told Olejniczak. "I shouldn't tell you this because you're liable to kick the crap out of us."

Once hired, Lombardi made it clear to the Packers' executive committee, which had given him control as both general manager and head coach, that the decisions were his and his alone. The committee agreed, and it may have been the best decision it ever made.

What Lombardi brought to the Pack was something the team had never seen before. He inspired fear and anger, he was intimidating and demanding, and in time, he would inspire the kind of devotion that has lasted for decades from many of his players.

CHICAGO BEARS
Official Program
PRICE 25¢
GREEN BAY CITY STADIUM
—VS.—
GREEN BAY PACKERS
SEPTEMBER 27th, 1959 • 1:06 P.M.

Above: *On September 27, 1959, Vince Lombardi made his debut as head coach of the Green Bay Packers, who slipped past the Chicago Bears 9–6.* **Below:** *"The Coach" is surrounded by his players during a November 1959 game.*

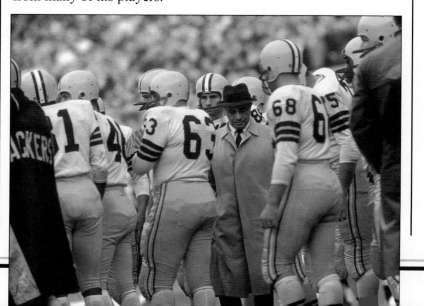

Packers coach Vince Lombardi outlines a play in the locker room during the 1963 season. During his time in Green Bay, Lombardi compiled a 105–35–6 record that included five NFL titles and two Super Bowl wins.

In an early meeting with his new team, Lombardi said that he would stress fundamentals. To illustrate this, he held up a football and said, "Gentlemen, this is a football." Veteran wide receiver and team jokester Max McGee interrupted, "Coach, could you slow down a little? You're going too fast for us."

McGee didn't interrupt like that again.

In the first meeting with his new team, Lombardi told his squad, "Gentlemen, we are always going to relentlessly chase perfection, knowing full well we will not catch it because nothing is perfect. In the process, we will catch excellence." After a brief pause, Lombardi looked at them and said, "I am not remotely interested in being just good."

After that meeting, Starr called his wife and told her that everything in Green Bay was changing. And change it did—immediately. In the first game of the 1959 season, the Packers beat the Bears 9–6, thanks to a late touchdown run by Jim Taylor. Hundreds of fans stormed the field as if the team had won a title.

A five-game losing streak in the middle of the season seemed to signal a return to the usual routine, but something was different. After that skid, the Packers pulled themselves together to close with four straight wins and a 7–5 record. It was Green Bay's first winning season since 1947.

For his efforts, Lombardi was named the 1959 NFL Coach of the Year. But a 7–5 record was nothing special in Lombardi's eyes. He knew there was still a lot of work to be done.

Lombardi Speaks

Even today, Vince Lombardi's quotes inspire athletes, business leaders, and politicians. Here are some of the great man's great words:

• "I don't think we have better players than anyone else. But we don't keep anyone here who doesn't become a part of the team. When a game is over, it's not how I did, but how the team did."

• "If it doesn't matter who wins or loses, then why do they keep score?"

• "Confidence is contagious. So is lack of confidence."

Vince Lombardi is well known for his coaching philosophy and his ability to motivate his players, who were fiercely devoted to him. His memorable quips are still frequently quoted to this day.

• "Coaches who can outline plays on a blackboard are a dime a dozen. The ones who win get inside their players and motivate."

• "Show me a good loser, and I'll show you a loser."

• "The real glory is being knocked to your knees and then coming back. That's real glory. That's the essence of it."

• "Leaders are made, they are not born."

• "We go on execution. We run a play and we run it and run it until our players like it."

• "Fatigue makes cowards of us all."

• "Winning isn't everything, it's the only thing."

PACKERS PARAPHERNALIA

THE SPORT OF THE '60s

THIRTY CENTS   DECEMBER 21, 1962

TIME
THE WEEKLY NEWSMAGAZINE

GREEN BAY COACH
VINCE LOMBARDI

VOL. LXXX NO. 25

Vince Lombardi appeared on the December 22, 1962, cover of *Time* magazine to represent football—"the sport of the '60s."

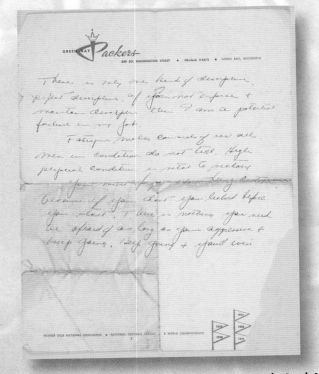

Vince Lombardi carried this speech in his wallet in 1959, his first year in Green Bay. In part, it reads, "There is nothing you need be afraid of as long as you're aggressive & keep going. Keep going & you'll win."

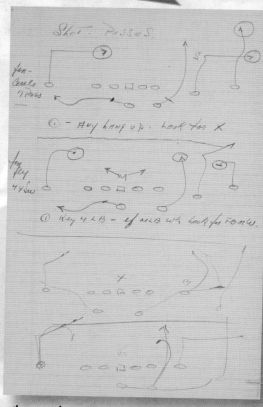

These handwritten diagrams outline some of Vince Lombardi's famous plays.

Mental attitude is 75% of winning.

Good fellows are a dime a dozen, but an aggressive leader is priceless

Winning is a habit.

Confidence is contagious. So is a lack of confidence.

Want it!   Desire it!   Earn it!   Take it!

Desire is a constant thing.

Desire is a cold fury burning inside a man.

There are only two or three plays in every game that decides who wins or loses. You never know when the key play is coming up.

You must force things to happen. You grab the initiative.

Anything is ours providing we are willing to pay the price.

The primary objective of the Green Bay Packers must be victory. It cannot be achieved by anything less than complete dedication.

Be quick or lose.

Vince Lombardi had some of his motivational quotes, such as these, scattered around the Packers' locker room to inspire his players to think positive, have confidence, pursue their desires, and above all else, win.

In this handwritten speech, entitled "What is Freedom," Vince Lombardi urges Americans not to take for granted the rights, privileges, and blessings bestowed upon them "simply by accident of birth."

This bobblehead captures the concentrated gaze of "The Coach."

This figurine portrays "The Coach" in classic style—wearing a suit, tie, and his trademark coat and fedora.

VINCE LOMBARDI'S GAME

The most realistic Pro Football Game ever developed!

On offense and defense, every player in both the NFL and AFL performs as he does in real-life ...and YOU make the decisions!

RGI*

VINCE LOMBARDI'S GAME

As general manager and head coach of the Green Bay Packers, Vince Lombardi signed his own paychecks.

Football fans tested their coaching acumen with Vince Lombardi's Game. The elaborate board game included rosters for each NFL team, "defensive play cards," an "offensive plays board," score sheets, time sheets, and yard markers.

Paul Hornung: The Golden Boy

If anyone besides Vince Lombardi had taken over as Green Bay's head coach in 1959, Paul Hornung might have slipped into history as just another Heisman Trophy winner who couldn't make it in the NFL.

Indeed, neither Lisle Blackbourn, who selected Hornung with the very first pick of the 1957 NFL draft, nor his successor, Ray McLean, could figure out what to do with "The Golden Boy." Although Hornung was a quarterback at Notre Dame, neither McLean nor Blackbourn thought he threw well enough to play the position in the NFL. At the same time, they didn't think he ran well enough to be a halfback.

Frustrated after two poor seasons, Hornung sought a trade. Then came Lombardi, who saw in Hornung a multifaceted offensive threat. The result was that for three years, Hornung was perhaps the NFL's most dangerous offensive weapon as a receiver, passer, runner, and kicker. From 1959 to 1961, he was the league's leading scorer; in 1960 alone, he racked up 176 points (13 rushing touchdowns, two touchdown passes, 41 extra points, and 15 field goals), an NFL record that still stands.

Heisman Trophy winner Paul Hornung was the first overall draft pick of 1957 and a multitalented quarterback, running back, and kicker, but, at first, the Packers weren't sure what to do with him.

But as gifted as Hornung was, no one really knows how good he could have been had he not missed an extended period in 1961 serving in the Army Reserve and, worse, the entire 1963 season due to his NFL-sanctioned suspension for gambling. Injuries plagued him later in his career and forced him to watch on the sidelines as the Packers brought home a victory in Super Bowl I in January 1967. Prior to the '67 season, Hornung was selected by the New Orleans Saints in the expansion draft, but due to nagging injuries, he retired before the season began.

Paul Hornung, the Packers' No. 4 all-time scorer, was inducted into the Packers Hall of Fame in 1975 and the Pro Football Hall of Fame in 1986.

Paul Hornung (5), seen here in the 1965 NFL championship game against the Cleveland Browns, rushed for 3,711 yards in his career.

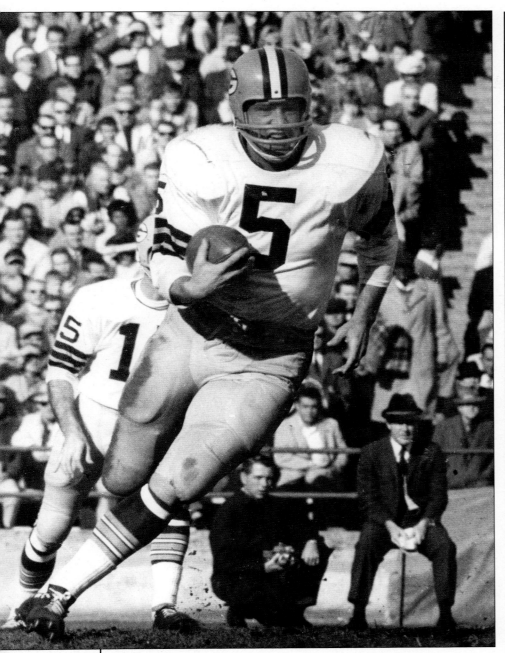

Nicknamed "The Golden Boy" during his days at Notre Dame, Paul Hornung was the NFL's Player of the Year in 1961. He racked up 760 points in his nine seasons as a Green Bay Packer.

It wasn't all fun and games for Paul Hornung, who was suspended for the 1963 season for gambling on sports. He admitted his guilt but insisted that he never bet on Packers games.

A Bad Bet

It was like a bolt of lightning from out of the blue, and it may have gone a long way toward keeping the Packers from winning another NFL championship. In April 1963, four months after the Packers beat the Giants for the 1962 title, NFL commissioner Pete Rozelle suspended both Paul Hornung and Detroit Lions defensive tackle Alex Karras for the entire 1963 season for betting on NFL games.

Hornung never denied the charges but insisted that gambling was rampant throughout the league. Nevertheless, the league was going to punish Hornung and Karras, two high-profile players, to set an example of what happens to those who engage in bad behavior.

The Packers didn't exactly struggle in 1963—they finished 11–2–1—but they still lost the Western Conference title to the Chicago Bears.

Hornung wasn't the same player when he returned in 1964, and a wide range of injuries—from back to neck to knee—began to take their toll on the "Golden Boy." He retired after the 1966 season.

Heartbreak in '60

Vince Lombardi had performed a minor miracle in 1959 by taking a forlorn team to a 7–5 record. It was the franchise's best record since 1944, and many Packers fans were quite pleased with that.

But Lombardi wasn't, and that's what separated him from other coaches. He expected to win every time he stepped onto the field, so posting five losses was unacceptable. As a result, he drove his team even harder the next season because he saw just how special this group could one day be.

The 1960 season started badly, as the Packers fell to the Bears 17–14 in the opener. Worse, Bart Starr, whom Lombardi had hoped would be his quarterback for years to come, played terribly. Without hesitation, Lombardi benched Starr in favor of Lamar McHan, who led the Packers to three straight wins. The move was surely a ploy to get Starr's attention—and it worked.

During the season's fifth game, with the Packers trailing the Pittsburgh Steelers in the final minutes, Lombardi reinserted

Starr, who led Green Bay on a 66-yard touchdown drive for the victory. Starr had his spot back, and he would not relinquish it again.

With a defense dominated by the fearsome Ray Nitschke at middle linebacker and an offense featuring Starr, Paul Hornung, Jim Taylor, and Max McGee, the 1960 Packers posted an 8–4 record, their best since 1944—the last time they'd won an NFL title. But as Lombardi made abundantly clear, the job wasn't done.

In the locker room after the 1960 title game, Vince Lombardi told his players they would never lose another championship game under his watch. They never did.

Green Bay had a chance for its first league title in 16 years, but the team would have to navigate past the tough Philadelphia Eagles at their home stadium, Franklin Field, in the championship game.

The Packers took a 6–0 lead in the second quarter on two Hornung field goals, but the Eagles rallied to take a 10–6 halftime lead, thanks in part to Norm Van Brocklin's 35-yard touchdown pass to Tommy McDonald.

The Packers regained the lead in the fourth quarter when Starr threw a seven-yard touchdown pass to McGee. But the Eagles went back ahead on Ted Dean's five-yard scoring run with five minutes left to play. The Packers fought back one more time, driving to the Eagles' 22-yard line. On the final play of the game, Starr threw a pass to Taylor, who was stopped at the Philly eight-yard line as time expired, giving the Eagles a 17–13 win and their third NFL title.

As disappointed as the Packers were, they knew that they had been in a special game. There were 67,000 fans in attendance in Philadelphia, and a huge TV audience watched at home. It was another step toward football taking its place as America's favorite sport, and the Packers figured to play a big role in this process.

Paul Hornung leaves the field with coach Vince Lombardi after the Eagles defeated the Packers 17–13 in the 1960 NFL championship game.

Starr Appeal

Perhaps no one flourished more under the tutelage of Vince Lombardi than Bart Starr. From the minute Lombardi took over as head coach, something clicked with Starr. He saw in Lombardi the man who could not only turn the Packers around, but could make him the player he knew he could be.

After playing for Bear Bryant at Alabama, Starr was drafted in the 17th-round of the 1956 draft. (In those days, the draft went on for 30 rounds.) He was unimpressive in his first three seasons with the Packers, throwing 13 touchdown passes and 25 interceptions during that time. But when Lombardi came on the scene in 1959, everything changed for Starr.

Lombardi made Starr his so-called "coach on the field," and the unflappable quarterback took it from there, leading the Packers to NFL titles in 1961, '62, '65, '66, and '67. He was the league's MVP in 1966 and was at the helm when the Packers won the first two Super Bowls; he was named the most valuable player of both games.

Starr's numbers were never gaudy, but he was always efficient. He threw for 24,718 yards and 152 touchdowns in his career, completing at least 52 percent of his passes every season except 1958 (49.7 percent). Starr epitomized the Lombardi-era Packers, and when Lombardi

Quarterback Bart Starr was the Packers' 17th-round draft pick in 1956. Vince Lombardi had total confidence in his QB and often referred to him as his "coach on the field."

left the sidelines after the 1967 season, Starr's role changed, too.

Though he continued as the starting quarterback, his supporting cast was changing, and the success the Packers had known for most of the decade was ending. By 1971, Starr was dealing with major health issues, including a scare prior to that season when he nearly bled to death while undergoing an experimental surgery to fix his ailing shoulder. He played just four games in 1971 and retired before training camp in 1972.

Always faithful to the Packers, Starr stayed on to help head coach Dan Devine tutor the quarterbacks in 1972 and then moved on to various careers that included TV work and car sales. In 1975, he again answered the Packers' call, accepting the head-coaching position even though he'd never been a head coach before. In nine seasons, he posted a 52–76–3 record with just two winning seasons. To this day, he politely refuses to discuss his coaching career in any detail.

Starr was inducted into both the Pro Football Hall of Fame and the Packers Hall of Fame in 1977.

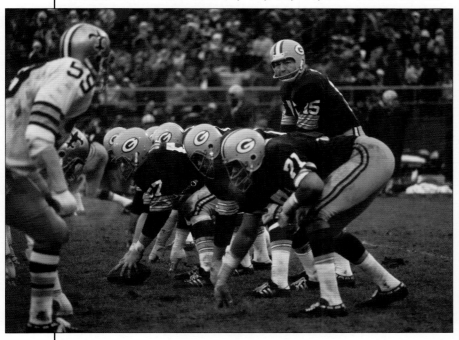

Bart Starr calls signals during a November 28, 1971, game against the New Orleans Saints. Battered by age and injuries, Starr retired at the end of the season.

The Pack Goes Back-to-Back

In the aftermath of an agonizing loss to the Philadelphia Eagles for the 1960 NFL title, Vince Lombardi gathered his team together and made a simple, dramatic statement: The Packers would never lose another championship game so long as he was the head coach.

"That was pretty strong talk," Willie Davis recalled. But as bold—some might say arrogant—as it was, it was also classic Lombardi. What else would he say? He believed so strongly in his players' talent and his ability as coach, and he abhorred losing so much, that it only made sense to say that if, and when, the Packers returned to a title game, they would win it.

They got their chance the very next season. The Packers rolled to an 11–3 record en route to a second straight Western Division

title, and found themselves back in the championship game—this time against the New York Giants and this time on their home turf.

Though Lombardi was confident, he was concerned that Paul Hornung, his leading scorer, might have to miss the final showdown because of his responsibilities in the Army Reserve, where he was a truck driver and radio operator at Fort Riley in Kansas. In the early 1960s, the Packers and the rest of the NFL often lost players to military assignments, as many were called to active duty due to escalating Cold War tensions.

But now it was crunch time, and, fortunately for the Packers, Vince Lombardi had a powerful ally. The coach put in a call to President John F. Kennedy, who arranged a weekend pass for Hornung so he could play against the Giants for the NFL crown.

Paul Hornung, shown here at Fort Riley in 1962, was scheduled to miss the NFL title game against the Giants. But Coach Lombardi pulled a few strings to get Hornung's assignment moved to a later date.

And it was no contest. Hornung scored 19 points on his own (one touchdown run, four extra points, and three field goals) as the Packers held the Giants to just 130 total yards and forced five turnovers to decimate New York 37–0 for their first NFL title since 1944.

"This is the greatest team in the history of the National Football League," Lombardi proclaimed at the time. But they were only getting started.

The Packers were back in '62 and were even better than the year before, coasting through the regular season with a 13–1 record. It was déjà vu as they faced the Giants in the title game

The victorious Packers carry coach Vince Lombardi off the field after beating the New York Giants 37–0 in the 1961 NFL championship game on December 31. It was Green Bay's first league title since 1944.

once again, but the New Yorkers had not forgotten how the Packers had humiliated them the year before in Green Bay.

"They wanted revenge," fullback Jim Taylor said.

And this time, the game was played at Yankee Stadium in New York, although the weather conditions that day rivaled those of Green Bay's "Frozen Tundra"—the temperature was 13 degrees and a constant 40-mile-per-hour wind whipped through the stadium. Perhaps the men from Green Bay were used to the frigid temps, because they prevailed. Right guard Jerry Kramer kicked three field goals, linebacker Ray Nitschke recovered two fumbles, and the battered Taylor ran for 85 yards and Green Bay's only touchdown as the Packers nabbed their second straight title with a 16–7 victory.

As several Packers looked back, they pointed to that 1962 championship as the crowning achievement of their careers. That's because the weather, the crowd, and the circumstances all conspired against Green Bay, but the Packers still found a way to win.

"It was just a hell of a football game," Kramer said.

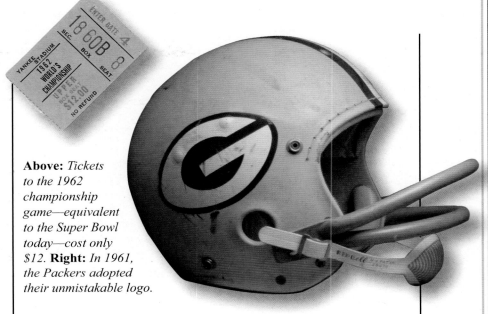

Above: *Tickets to the 1962 championship game—equivalent to the Super Bowl today—cost only $12.* **Right:** *In 1961, the Packers adopted their unmistakable logo.*

Packers fullback Jim Taylor (31) barrels in for a touchdown during the NFL title game against the New York Giants on December 30, 1962. Green Bay won the game 16–7 to nail down the team's eighth NFL championship.

A White Letter Day

It's as identifiable a part of the Green Bay Packers' mystique as the green and gold uniforms, Lambeau Field, and those ubiquitous cheeseheads.

It is the simple, stark, elegant, white block *G* that rests on a forest green background on the yellow-gold helmet. Nearly everyone, even those who don't know the difference between a football and a baseball, recognizes it.

The simple logo was designed and introduced in 1961 by Packers equipment manager George "Dad" Braisher, and it has remained essentially untouched ever since. As with most professional sports logos, it is trademarked, and with a few exceptions (i.e., the University of Georgia, Grambling State University), it can't be duplicated without permission.

In the early '90s, general manager Ron Wolf briefly considered slightly altering the team colors, but he knew better than to mess with the *G*. And when he saw some prospective designs, he quickly changed his mind. He learned that you don't fix what isn't broken.

PACKERS PARAPHERNALIA

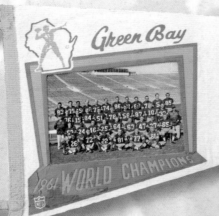

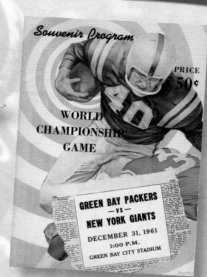

The Packers blanked the New York Giants 37–0 on December 31, 1961, to nail down their seventh NFL title.

Packers fans were proud to display pennants like this one, which holds a photo of the 1961 world champions.

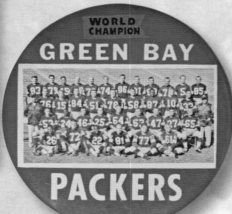

Vince Lombardi shows off a congratulatory telegram he received from an admirer—President John F. Kennedy.

Proud Packer Backers kept their favorite team close to their hearts with buttons like this one, which depicts the '61 champs.

On January 1, 1962, it was front-page news throughout Wisconsin when the Packers were declared world champs once again.

This football commemorates the Packers' 16-7 victory over the Giants in the 1962 NFL championship game.

A 1963 team schedule shows that the Packers were still basking in the glory of their '62 NFL title.

The white block G is synonymous with the Green Bay Packers and has been since 1961.

Packers fans have always been loyal. But they were eager to show their pride in the early '60s, after more than a decade of drought.

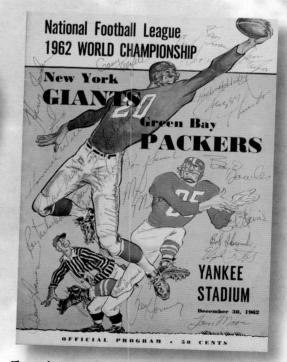

For the second straight year, the Packers knocked off the New York Giants to win the NFL championship.

The 1965 Championship: A Close Call

Although the Packers posted 11–2–1 and 8–5–1 records in 1963 and 1964, respectively, those seasons were considered failures in Vince Lombardi's mind for no other reason than the Packers failed to return to the NFL championship game.

In 1965, the Packers finally righted their ship, finishing 10–3–1, which left them tied with the Baltimore Colts for the Western Conference championship. That led to a tie-breaking game against the Colts on December 26 at the newly christened Lambeau Field. It was one of the strangest postseason games ever played.

Because of injuries, the Colts had to play without either of their quarterbacks—Johnny Unitas and Gary Cuozzo—which forced halfback Tom Matte into the role. The Packers also had to overcome the loss of their QB, Bart Starr, due to an injury early in the game. The Pack came back from a 10–0 halftime deficit to tie things up with less than two minutes left in regulation play, when Don Chandler kicked a 25-yard field goal that Colts fans still insist was wide right. (The controversy prompted the NFL to lengthen the uprights the following season.) This divisive play forced overtime—a first in Packers playoff history—and Green Bay went on to win 13–10. They were one step closer to another NFL title, but they'd have to get past the Cleveland Browns in the championship game first.

Green Bay was the recipient of four inches of snow on game day, which helped to soften the field. Perhaps

Jim Taylor (31) carries the ball during the 1965 NFL title game against the Cleveland Browns on January 2, 1966. Taylor was a workhorse in the 23–12 victory, carrying the ball 27 times for 86 yards.

Dedication and Devotion

The concept of tailgating may not have been invented in Green Bay, but it was very likely perfected there.

In an era in which the Packers were pro football's top team and likely one of the most recognizable sports teams in the country, Packers fans couldn't get enough. They took to showing up for games early—really early—to set up grills, crack open some beverages, and basically just enjoy the day. Now, it's practically a requirement at Packers home games.

During the 1960s and early '70s, the inimitable Golden Girls—a collection of high school and college cheerleaders who danced, twirled batons, and generally revved up the fans—provided entertainment from the sidelines. It was a far cry from what NFL teams provide today, but in the simpler days of this era, they were perfect for the Packers. They most notably earned admiration for their hardiness while entertaining frozen fans during the "Ice Bowl," a game in which several of the Golden Girls suffered minor frostbite. Now *that's* devotion.

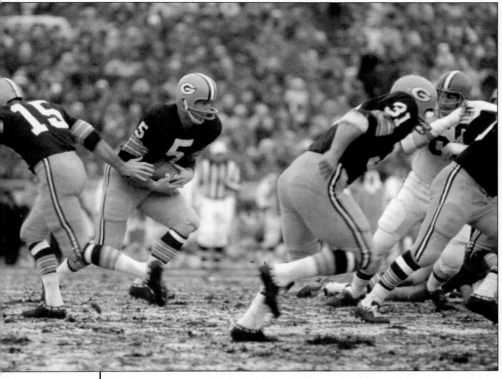

Bart Starr (15) hands the ball to Paul Hornung (5), who rushed for 105 yards and a touchdown as the Packers edged the Cleveland Browns for the 1965 NFL championship, the ninth title in franchise history.

that's why Cleveland's star back Jim Brown couldn't get much traction and was held to just 50 rushing yards.

It was a tight game, but the Packers eventually put it away with an 11-play, 90-yard drive in the third quarter that ended with a Paul Hornung touchdown run and sealed a 23–12 victory for Green Bay.

In seven seasons under Lombardi, it was Green Bay's third NFL title.

On December 26, 1965, the Packers faced the Baltimore Colts in a playoff game to decide the Western Conference champ. The Pack's 13–10 win meant a showdown with the Cleveland Browns for the NFL title.

Above: *The Golden Girls often wore gold sequined outfits like this one, which belonged to the squad's founding member, Mary Jane Sorgel.*
Left: *From 1961 to 1972, the Golden Girls were the Packers' official cheerleaders.*

A Forrest of a Man

A second-round draft pick for the Packers in 1956, Alvis Forrest Gregg was one of the first and most important pieces of the puzzle that became the Green Bay Packers dynasty of the 1960s.

Gregg took his spot at right tackle for the Packers in 1958 (after missing the 1957 season to serve in the Army) and did not leave the lineup until 1970, playing in a then-record 187 straight games.

At 6′4″ and 250 pounds, Gregg was considered undersized for a lineman, even in those days. But his quickness, technique, and intelligence made him perhaps the most indispensable lineman on a team that also included the likes of Bob Skoronski, Fuzzy Thurston, Gale Gillingham, Jerry Kramer, and Ken Bowman. In his book *Run to Daylight,* Vince Lombardi referred to Gregg as "the finest player I ever coached."

Gregg was the linchpin on a Packers line that won five NFL championships and two Super Bowls in the 1960s. He was named All-Pro eight times, including selections at both guard and tackle

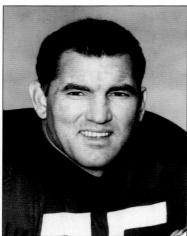

Legendary coach Vince Lombardi once called Hall of Famer Forrest Gregg "the finest player I ever coached."

in 1965. Gregg was also a nine-time Pro Bowler and was voted to the NFL's 75th anniversary team in 1994. He ended his career in 1971 with the Dallas Cowboys, helping them secure a victory in Super Bowl VI.

After his playing days ended, Gregg became an assistant coach, first with the San Diego Chargers and then with the Cleveland Browns, where he took the reins as head coach at the end of the 1974 season and stayed until he was fired in 1977. After a stint in the Canadian

Forrest Gregg leaves the field during the 1965 NFL championship game against the Cleveland Browns. A few inches of snow earlier in the day had softened up Lambeau Field and turned the game into a mudfest.

Football League, he returned to the NFL in 1980, where he took over as head coach of the Cincinnati Bengals, whom he led to Super Bowl XVI, a 26–21 loss to the San Francisco 49ers.

Like so many former Packers, Gregg answered Green Bay's call, and, in 1984, he took over for his old teammate, Bart Starr, as head coach. But Gregg's tenure was marred by disciplinary issues that included legal problems for several players. His first two teams both went 8–8, but then his Packers tumbled to 4–12 in 1986 and 5–9–1 in 1987. He resigned after that season to take over the football program at his alma mater, Southern Methodist University, a team that was trying to rebound from major NCAA infractions. He coached there for two years and then became SMU's athletic director.

Gregg was inducted into both the Pro Football Hall of Fame and the Packers Hall of Fame in 1977.

Taylor-Made for Football

Norm Van Brocklin, the star quarterback of the Philadelphia Eagles during the 1950s, once said of Green Bay Packers fullback Jim Taylor: "He's tougher than Japanese arithmetic."

Presumably, that was a compliment.

Indeed, in an era of tough guys, few were tougher than Taylor, the former LSU star with the crew-cut and the busted nose who never looked like he ran that hard but always seemed to punish anyone who tried to tackle him.

In the NFL of the 1960s, fullback was the premier position. The fullback was the guy who had to run for the tough yards, block, and catch passes, and from 1958 to 1966, Taylor was a huge part of the Packers' ground attack. Paul Hornung may have been more versatile, but when tough yards were needed, it was Taylor who provided them. He led the Packers in rushing seven straight seasons (1960–66), and had five straight 1,000-yard seasons (1960–64). In fact, when he gained 1,101 yards on the ground in 1960, it marked the first time that a Packer had rushed for more than 1,000 yards since Tony Canadeo in 1949. Through the end of the 2008 season, Taylor's mark of 8,207 career rushing yards remained a club record, and his single-season record of 1,474 yards (set in 1962) remained intact until Ahman Green surpassed it with 1,883 in 2003. And he did it all while looking as though he wasn't even running that hard.

Taylor was also known for two feuds: one with New York Giants linebacker Sam Huff and the other with his own coach. The first is a classic story from the 1962 NFL title game in New York.

After one especially rugged tackle, Huff loomed over Taylor and said simply, "Taylor, you stink." Later in the game, after Taylor scored a touchdown, he yelled to Huff, "Hey Sam, how do I smell from here?"

Taylor also had a scratchy relationship with Lombardi. When he negotiated his first deal under the venerable coach, Taylor wanted $9,500 with a $1,000 bonus. Lombardi paid it, but he demanded even more from Taylor in return. By the end of the 1966 season, the constant pounding had finally caught up to Taylor. After another turbulent contract negotiation with Lombardi in 1967, Taylor signed with the expansion New Orleans Saints, who were delighted to have a native son return home. Taylor played one more season and then retired. He was inducted into the Packers Hall of Fame in 1975 and the Pro Football Hall of Fame in 1976.

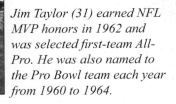

Jim Taylor (31) earned NFL MVP honors in 1962 and was selected first-team All-Pro. He was also named to the Pro Bowl team each year from 1960 to 1964.

Jim Taylor rushed for more than 8,000 yards and scored 83 touchdowns in nine seasons with the Green Bay Packers.

Mr. Linebacker: Ray Nitschke

Ray Nitschke was a walking, talking, quarterback-hunting enigma. One of the meanest and best linebackers in NFL history, he would destroy opponents and then loom over them, relishing the hit.

But off the field, he was one of the gentlest, kindest souls one could imagine. Nevertheless, he looked the part of pure evil on the football field—bald-headed with a craggy face, a prominent nose, and a smile that showed he was missing his two front teeth. He was everywhere on the football field, knocking down passes, making tackles, and dominating the game in a way that few middle linebackers could.

So tough was Nitschke that when a metal tower once fell on him during practice, Coach Lombardi looked at him and told his players to get back to work. "He's all right," Lombardi scoffed. (Actually, a jagged piece of metal did pierce Nitschke's helmet, barely missing his skull. The helmet is still on display at the Packers Hall of Fame.)

Ray Nitschke, a fan favorite who played for the Packers from 1958 to 1972, was one of the most feared linebackers in the NFL.

Nitschke, a third-round pick for the Packers in 1958, hailed from the University of Illinois. And like many Packers of his era, he didn't really flourish in Green Bay until Lombardi arrived. He became the Packers' starting middle linebacker in 1960 and was a mainstay until his retirement in 1972. He finished his Packers career with 25 interceptions, and his 20 career fumble recoveries still rank second in team history behind Willie Davis's 21.

A five-time All-Pro and a Pro Bowler in 1964, Nitschke was named to the NFL's 50th and 75th Anniversary teams. He played 190 games for the Packers—third-most in team history—and his No. 66 was retired in 1983; it was only the fourth number in club history (at the time) to be retired. Other Packer greats who have had their numbers retired include: Tony Canadeo (3), Don Hutson (14), Bart Starr (15), and Reggie White (92).

Nitschke was so beloved by Packers fans that they were outraged when coach Dan Devine replaced him with Jim Carter as the starting middle linebacker in 1971. Indeed, fans were ruthless with Carter, who was a perfectly adequate player but had no chance with Packer Backers simply because he was not Nitschke.

Nitschke was inducted into both the Pro Football Hall of Fame and the Packers Hall of Fame in 1978. Despite his ferocious on-field persona, Nitschke had a soft spot for kids and special causes. He made Green Bay his home after retiring from football and always kept his name listed in the local phone book. As an unabashed Packers fan, he suffered with everyone else during the lean years, and when they won the Super Bowl in '96, he wept at the team's parade. He died two years later at age 61.

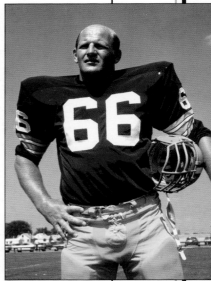

The fans loved Ray Nitschke, who remained close to the Packers for the rest of his life.

Stars of the Era

For **Willie Davis,** being traded from the Cleveland Browns to the Packers in 1960 for someone named A. D. Williams was the best thing that ever happened to him. Davis settled in at left defensive end and didn't leave for a decade. He was a five-time Pro Bowler and a five-time All-Pro who never missed a game in 12 seasons. He still holds the team record for fumble recoveries with 21.

Willie Davis said that being traded to the Packers from the Cleveland Browns was the best thing that ever happened to him.

Davis retired after the 1969 season, then utilized the MBA he earned from the University of Chicago to become a successful businessman in Southern California. He was inducted into the Packers Hall of Fame in 1975 and the Pro Football Hall of Fame in 1981.

Herb Adderley, Green Bay's first-round draft choice in 1961, was a five-time All-Pro, a five-time Pro Bowler, and one of the game's first truly dominant cornerbacks. He finished his Packers career with 39 interceptions, seven of which he returned for touchdowns. He was traded to the Dallas Cowboys in 1970 and proceeded to lead them to two Super Bowls. He was inducted into the Pro Football Hall of Fame in 1980 and the Packers Hall of Fame in 1981.

Herb Adderley was a star running back at Michigan State, but he quickly became a defensive specialist at cornerback for the Packers.

Jerry Kramer, perhaps the most famous lineman on a team of famous linemen, is best known for instigating the famous block that sprung Bart Starr loose for the winning touchdown in the 1967 "Ice Bowl." He also kicked three field goals in the 1962 NFL title game and anchored a line that dominated the league in the mid-1960s.

Kramer played for the Packers from 1958 to 1968, but he battled injuries for years, which may have cut his career short. Nevertheless, he was a six-time All-Pro and was named to the Packers All-Time Modern Era team, All-Century team, and 50th Anniversary team. He was inducted into the Packers Hall of Fame in 1975.

After he left football, Kramer became a best-selling author, penning books such as *Instant Replay* and *Distant Replay*. One day, he hopes to write a screenplay about the Lombardi-era Packers.

From 1953 to 1963, **Jim Ringo** was the Packers' preeminent center. He was traded to the Philadelphia Eagles in 1964 and retired after the '67 season. He was an eight-time All-Pro (seven in Green Bay) and went to ten Pro Bowls (seven as a Packer). From 1953 to 1967, Ringo played in 182 straight games, including 126 straight with the Packers.

Ringo was inducted into the Packers Hall of Fame in 1974 and the Pro Football Hall of Fame in 1981.

Above: *Despite his lofty statistics, Jerry Kramer is still awaiting enshrinement in Canton.*
Below: *Jim Ringo became an integral part of the Lombardi Sweep, but he almost quit football as a rookie.*

PACKERS PARAPHERNALIA

A red circle marks the puncture left by a metal tower that fell on Ray Nitschke during a practice session and nearly pierced the linebacker's skull.

The Ray Nitschke bobblehead can take a whack to the noggin and bounce back for more.

Above: This poster from the 1960s highlights some of the greatest Packers in team history.

We LOVE Ray 66

Fans loved Ray Nitschke for his tough, on-field persona, as well as his kindness and generosity off the field.

Before VHS tapes and DVDs, memorable seasons were commemorated on albums such as this one, which salutes the Packers' three-peat in the late 1960s.

GREEN BAY PACKERS

This action-packed pennant captured the excitement and enthusiasm of Packers football during the 1960s.

The 1950s weren't exactly the glory years for the Bears or the Packers, but that didn't cool their heated rivalry.

OFFICIAL PROGRAM 35 CENTS
WRIGLEY FIELD NOVEMBER 7, 1954

CHICAGO BEARS vs. GREEN BAY PACKERS

In this campy sticker, a player packs footballs in a Packers crate. "Kitsch" has long been a part of Packers culture.

Bobblehead dolls like these, which depict Packers players and Golden Girls cheerleaders, gained popularity in the 1960s and are sought-after collectibles today.

Elijah Pitts (22) played for the Packers for ten seasons. He led the team in kickoff returns in 1965 and in punt returns in '69.

Bart Starr received this trophy for being the NFL's most valuable player in 1966.

Super Bowl I

In June 1966, the NFL called a truce with its most dangerous rival yet—the upstart American Football League (AFL). Since 1960, the AFL had given the NFL a run for its money by playing a brand of wide-open, exciting football that was different from the NFL and had thrilled fans and, more importantly, put people in the seats.

More to the point, the AFL was also doing a decent job of luring NFL players and convincing hotshot college stars—like Alabama quarterback Joe Namath—to sign with its teams. So, to quell the rivalry, NFL commissioner Pete Rozelle proposed a merger between the two leagues that would allow each to keep its identity but would ultimately lead to one, unified entity. It would also lead to a real championship game, with the best of the NFL facing the best of the AFL.

As the reigning kings of the NFL, the Packers felt pressured to demonstrate their league's superiority. Nevertheless, they cruised through the 1966 season, posting a 12–2 record and beating the Dallas Cowboys 34–27 for the NFL championship.

It was one of Bart Starr's greatest games—he threw four touchdown passes, including one to Max McGee late to put the contest away. But unlike in years past, when the Packers would have celebrated yet another title, the job wasn't quite done.

Instead, something called the "AFL–NFL World Championship Game" was to be played on January 15, 1967. The Packers would uphold the NFL's honor against the best of the AFL— the Kansas City Chiefs—at the Los Angeles Memorial Coliseum.

Vince Lombardi and his troops prepare to take on the Kansas City Chiefs in Super Bowl I. With the NFL's reputation at stake, Coach Lombardi was more nervous than he'd ever been.

Vince Lombardi and his players knew from the start that they had little to gain from this matchup. If the Packers won—and they were 14-point favorites—they would only have done what they were expected to do. If they lost? That thought was too terrible to contemplate.

As a result, Lombardi later stated that he had never been more nervous than he was for that game. Several Packers players admitted feeling the same way. "The thought of losing made me sick," linebacker Dave Robinson said.

They knew that a loss would shatter not only the league's image but also the carefully crafted image the Packers had built over time—that they were the best team the NFL had ever seen.

And so, before a crowd of 62,000—which barely filled half the Coliseum—the Chiefs played the Packers hard, trailing just 14–10 at

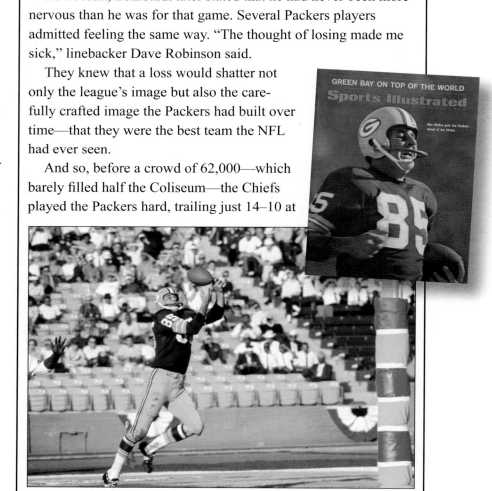

Max McGee (85) didn't expect to play in Super Bowl I, but when Boyd Dowler was injured, McGee grabbed the spotlight. Here, he catches one of two touchdown passes. He grabbed seven passes total for 138 yards.

Boyd Dowler (86) sails in for a touchdown against the Dallas Cowboys during the 1966 NFL championship game. The Packers won 34–27, which sent them to Super Bowl I to face the AFL's Kansas City Chiefs.

Bowled Over

It was supposed to be a joke. But an off-hand comment turned an uncertain new event into one of the true spectacles of pro sports.

In 1966, when the NFL and AFL agreed to merge, the deal was contingent on a true football championship between the two leagues. Originally, this championship game was given the clunky moniker the "AFL–NFL World Championship Game." But when AFL cofounder and Kansas City Chiefs owner Lamar Hunt saw his kids playing with a small rubber ball called a Super Ball, he suggested, with tongue in cheek, that the game be called the "Super Bowl."

NFL commissioner Pete Rozelle hated the name, but fans and the media loved it, so it stuck.

By the next season, when the Packers faced the Oakland Raiders for the championship, the game was officially known as the Super Bowl. Today, football fans can't imagine it being called anything else.

halftime. What surprised everyone was the player who caught the game's first touchdown pass—Max McGee. Once the Packers' top receiver, the aging McGee had been relegated to a backup role and had caught just four passes all season. But after an early injury to starting wide receiver Boyd Dowler, McGee was thrust back into the spotlight.

The story goes that McGee was so convinced that he wouldn't play in the game that he rather completely enjoyed the L.A. night-life the evening before. He admits that he rolled into his hotel room around 7:30 A.M. on game day.

Now he was front and center, and he responded with seven receptions for 138 yards and two touchdowns as Green Bay coasted past the Chiefs 35–10. Starr completed 16 of 23 passes for 250 yards and was named the game's most valuable player.

It was an impressive showing by the Packers and, in turn, the NFL, but Lombardi had little time to enjoy it because people were already starting to question whether the Packers could win a third straight title the following season.

Vince Lombardi accepts the Super Bowl trophy from NFL commissioner Pete Rozelle after the Packers defeated the Chiefs 35–10. Just a few years later, the trophy would be renamed in Lombardi's honor.

PACKERS PARAPHERNALIA

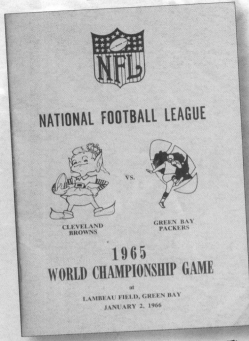

A pamphlet from the 1965 NFL title game portrays the Packers' opponents— the Cleveland Browns—as menacing elflike creatures.

The '85 Bears may have had the "Super Bowl Shuffle," but in the late 1960s, the "Packer Polka" was released to rally Green Bay fans.

The 1965 world championship game would mark the last year for the contest. Starting the next year, the Super Bowl would decide the best team in football.

As this pennant shows, the Packers played home games in both Green Bay and Milwaukee—an arrangement that lasted from 1933 to 1994.

This football commemorates the Packers' 23–12 victory over the Cleveland Browns, which made them NFL champs once again.

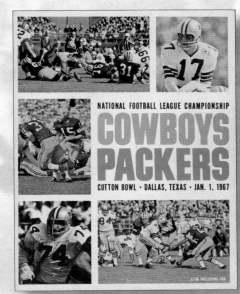

Before they made it to Super Bowl 1, the Packers had to get past the Dallas Cowboys to secure the NFL title. They did with a 34–27 win.

We know it as Super Bowl 1, but this program and ticket show that it was billed as the "AFL-NFL World Championship Game." Whatever you call it, the Packers won their tenth world title.

On January 2, 1967, the *Milwaukee Sentinel* announced that the Packers had won the NFL title. Two weeks later, they were hailed as world champs after their Super Bowl victory over the Kansas City Chiefs.

The city of Green Bay proudly presented the world champion Packers with this trophy in honor of their victory in Super Bowl 1 on January 15, 1967.

These footballs signify the route the Packers took on the way to their victory in Super Bowl 1 and their tenth NFL title.

The "Ice Bowl" and Super Bowl II

sk any Green Bay Packers fan of a certain age and he or she will tell you that they were sitting at Lambeau Field on December 31, 1967, that godforsaken day when NFL history, of a sort, was made.

Of course, they weren't all there, but it was still a sellout crowd of more than 50,000 fans who braved the –13 degree temperature to watch the aging, injured Packers take out the up-and-coming Dallas Cowboys for the NFL title.

The game will forever be known as the "Ice Bowl," but to the players who were there, it was simply a lesson in survival. The game has taken on mythical proportions for so many reasons, not the least of which was that it would be Vince Lombardi's last game at Lambeau Field, the last playoff game at Lambeau Field for 15 years, and the beginning of the end of another golden era in Packers history.

This was a Packers team in the midst of big changes. Jim Taylor was gone and many other stars were beat up and nearing the ends of their stellar careers. Bart Starr, coming off a Super Bowl MVP performance against the Chiefs, was awful in 1967, throwing just nine touchdown passes and 17 interceptions. Green Bay still posted a 9–4–1 record, but it was a drop-off from the past two seasons.

In the Western Conference championship game, the Packers beat the Los Angeles Rams 28–7, thanks to two touchdown runs by rookie Travis Williams and a swarming defense. This set up an NFL title game rematch against the Cowboys.

What many people forget is that the day before the "Ice Bowl," the weather was actually tolerable—well, at least for Green Bay

Vince Lombardi, seen here during the "Ice Bowl," remains a mythic figure in football and with his former players, who still refer to him as "Coach."

in December. And although the temperature hovered around zero degrees, there was no wind and the field was in excellent shape. But a cold front moved in overnight, damaging the state-of-the-art heating system that had recently been installed under Lambeau Field's turf.

Game day dawned brutally cold, and conditions were only made worse by a stiff wind that dropped windchills to a jarring –46 degrees. But the Packers seemed not to notice the weather, as they jumped to an early 14–0 lead on two Starr-to-Boyd Dowler

Above: *Despite subzero wind-chills, fans still packed Lambeau to watch the Packers battle the Cowboys for the 1967 NFL title.*
Below: *Bart Starr sneaks in for a touchdown to win the "Ice Bowl" and the NFL crown.*

Packers running back Donny Anderson (44) plows through for a touch-down in Super Bowl II. Green Bay coasted past the Oakland Raiders 33–14 for the victory and the 11th championship in franchise history.

touchdown passes. But Dallas climbed back into the game when George Andrie returned a Starr fumble for a touchdown and Danny Villanueva kicked a field goal, cutting the deficit to 14–10 at halftime.

On the first play of the fourth quarter, the Cowboys took the lead on Dan Reeves's 50-yard pass to Lance Rentzel, and, for the first time, some of the Packers wondered if their remarkable run was over. "I was thinking that maybe it wasn't meant to be," guard Jerry Kramer later recalled.

But with less than five minutes left in the game and the ball on Green Bay's 32-yard line, the Packers set off on an epic drive that would define this special team. "Everyone knew exactly what was at stake and what would be required," Starr said.

Using backs Donny Anderson and Chuck Mercein, the Packers drove to the Cowboys' 1-yard line. On third down, with just 13 seconds to play, Starr called a timeout to confer with Lombardi. Starr told his coach that he could use a wedge play to sneak into the end zone. Lombardi responded with words that Starr remembers to this day. "Well, run it, and let's get the hell out of here," the venerable coach grumbled.

Starr kept the play to himself, simply telling his linemen to get some footing. Starr was able to wedge himself over Kramer and center Ken Bowman and into the end zone to secure a 21–17 win.

Afterward, Bowman quipped, "It was probably the most famous play in the most famous game ever played, and only one of the 11 guys who ran it knew what was going on."

The Packers' victory set up what is generally considered an anticlimactic Super Bowl II on January 14, 1968, against the Oakland Raiders in Miami. The Packers took care of business, winning 33–14, but the victory was somewhat bittersweet—it was already known by most players and many fans that this was likely Lombardi's last game on the sidelines. And so, Kramer encouraged his teammates, "Let's win this for the old man."

Starr was again named the Super Bowl MVP, and the Packers again demonstrated the dominance of the NFL over the AFL, but most Packers faithful knew that something was about to change. Two weeks later, Lombardi made the announcement that everyone expected, when he retired from coaching due to poor health. Phil Bengtson, his trusted assistant, replaced him as head coach, and Lombardi stayed on as general manager.

It was the end of one incredible run.

Jerry Kramer carries coach Vince Lombardi off the field after winning Super Bowl II. It would be Lombardi's last game as Packers head coach.

The "Ice Bowl" is one of the most iconic games in Packers history. Despite the frigid weather conditions, the Green and Gold staged a dramatic, come-from-behind victory in the final seconds to clinch the NFL title.

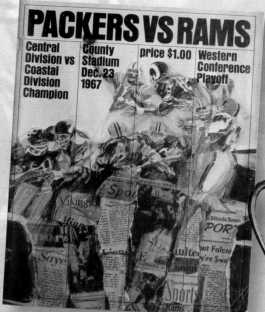

In the '67 Western Conference championship game, the Rams scored first, but it was all Packers after that. They won 28-7.

Fans were ecstatic—and rightfully so—over their Green Bay Packers, who won three world championships in a row in the late 1960s.

In addition to the trophy issued by the NFL, the city of Green Bay also gave the Packers this special memento for their Super Bowl II victory.

AFL VS NFL
1968 WORLD CHAMPIONSHIP GAME

The Packers met the Oakland Raiders in Miami for Super Bowl II on January 14, 1968. The price for a Super Bowl ticket in 1968—$12.

MILWAUKEE SENTINEL

★ ★ ★ ★ ★ FINAL

MONDAY MORNING, JANUARY 15, 1968

48 PAGES—3 PARTS

TEN CENTS

COLDER
Cloudy, chance of snow Sunday, colder Monday. High around 20. Low about 5. Maps, tables, page 18, part 2.

TODAY'S CHUCKLE
Learn from the snowflake. No two are alike, yet they work together beautifully on big jobs like tying up traffic.

Oakland Raiders Routed, 33-14
PACKERS STILL CHAMPS

For Green Bay Fans in Miami, It's Super

Over 5,000 From State At Game

Kasperak Is Operated On Again

US Mounts

The front page of the Milwaukee Sentinel from January 15, 1968, says it all. The Packers were world champs for the third straight year.

Sports Illustrated
JANUARY 22, 1968
THE SUPER CHAMPION
LOMBARDI OF GREEN BAY

This iconic photo of Jerry Kramer holding up Coach Lombardi after the Packers won Super Bowl II graced the January 22, 1968, cover of *Sports Illustrated*.

GREEN BAY PACKERS
WORLD CHAMPS

World Championship Game
AFL NFL
MIAMI FLORIDA
SUPER BOWL II

WORLD CHAMPIONS
JAN. 14, 1968
"THE DUKE"
PACKERS 33 RAIDERS 14

Fans were proud to display mementos like this sticker that declared the Pack world champs (left) and this patch from Super Bowl II.

This football was given to the Packers to commemorate their victory in Super Bowl II—the team's 11th world championship.

THE LEAN YEARS
1968–1991

THE "PACK" WILL BE BACK!

MARTHA'S COFFEE CLUB   ROMO DISPLAY ADV. GREEN BAY, WIS.

"The Green Bay Packers never lost a football game. They just ran out of time."

VINCE LOMBARDI

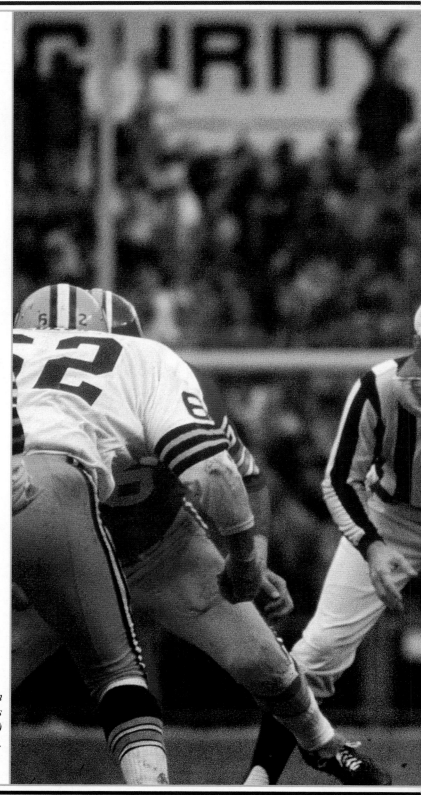

Above: *Although the Golden Age of the Green Bay Packers had clearly passed, fans never lost faith in their team, as is evidenced by stickers such as this one.* **Right:** *On November 26, 1972, the Packers squared off against the Washington Redskins at RFK Stadium. Here, quarterback Jerry Tagge (17) prepares to hand the ball to running back John Brockington (42) in the 21–16 Packers loss.*

Following a Legend

Throughout most of the 1967 season, even as the Packers were steaming toward a third straight NFL title, a storm was brewing. It was no secret that Vince Lombardi was looking for a new challenge and that his health was declining. So two weeks after Green Bay beat Oakland in Super Bowl II, it was no surprise that Lombardi announced his retirement from coaching.

As expected, Lombardi's successor was longtime defensive assistant Phil Bengtson, a nice guy who, as it turned out, was totally unprepared for what was to come. He was replacing a legend on the sidelines—that was bad enough. But Lombardi retained his general manager duties, so during every game, he would watch from high above Lambeau Field and scrutinize every move his protégé made. Several reporters from the era recall hearing Lombardi thunder from his personal box, "What the hell was *that*?"

The Packers stumbled in 1968—the first season post-Lombardi—managing just a 6–7–1 record a year after winning the Super Bowl. Meanwhile, the old coach was making plans to move on.

Lombardi had been talking with the forlorn Washington Redskins about becoming their head coach/general manager/vice president and part-owner. And on February 5, 1969, the end finally came when Lombardi left the Packers for the Redskins.

Lombardi was hailed as a savior by the Redskins and their fans, who hoped he could do for them what he'd done for the Packers. And in his one season in Washington, Lombardi did indeed perform some magic, taking the Redskins to a 7–5–2 record, their best mark since 1955.

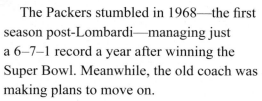

Phil Bengtson (left) was Vince Lombardi's handpicked successor as head coach, but with Lombardi still hovering as general manager, Bengtson never really had a chance to succeed.

But Packers fans were furious at Lombardi's departure. They felt betrayed and insulted that, after ten seasons, he would leave the place that made him famous. The 1960s had been good to the Packers, but a new decade was looming and the team's prospects weren't promising.

In 1969, Packers fans put their faith in Phil Bengtson, who took the team to an 8–6 record.

Saying Goodbye

Green Bay Packers fans seethed for a year as they watched Vince Lombardi turn the Washington Redskins around in much the same way he had revitalized the Packers ten years earlier. The hurt and anger, and perhaps a little jealousy, ran deep and strong.

But a thunderbolt that struck during the summer of 1970 zapped them back to reality. Lombardi was deathly ill with advanced colon cancer, and, on September 3, 1970, the great coach died in Washington, D.C., at age 57. More than 3,500 mourners attended his funeral in New York, and three of his favorite players—Bart Starr, Paul Hornung, and Willie Davis—were among his pallbearers. Lombardi was buried at Mount Olivet Cemetery in Middletown, New Jersey.

Three days after his funeral, NFL commissioner Pete Rozelle announced that, from then on, the trophy given to winners of the Super Bowl would be named after the legendary coach.

The NFL lost a legend in September 1970, when Vince Lombardi died of colon cancer. Here, pallbearers carry Lombardi's casket into St. Patrick's Cathedral in New York City.

Will the Pack Be Back?

Call it the last gasp of a dying empire. It was 1969, the end of a terrific decade that saw the Green Bay Packers win five championships, including the first two Super Bowls. From 1960 to 1967, the Packers won six division titles and finished second twice. And over the course of the decade, the Packers seared themselves into the national sports consciousness as a franchise that won with skill, class, and dedication.

But all that started to change in 1968, when Vince Lombardi—the architect of that dynasty—stepped off the sidelines.

In 1968, under Phil Bengtson, the Packers limped to the finish line with a 6–7–1 record, the team's first losing season since 1958—the year before Lombardi arrived in Green Bay. It was one of those transitional, often painful, seasons that proud franchises must go through as they pass from one phase to another.

But there were many in Green Bay, including several players, who didn't think that the run of greatness had to end just because Lombardi was gone. After all, many of the stars who were responsible for that success were still around, including quarterback Bart Starr; running backs Donny Anderson, Jim Grabowski, and Elijah Pitts; receivers Boyd Dowler and Carroll Dale; offensive linemen Forrest Gregg and Ken Bowman; and defensive stalwarts Ray Nitschke, Dave Robinson, Willie Wood, Herb Adderley, and Willie Davis.

So in 1969, the Packers saw an opportunity to recapture the magic and prove that time was not the enemy. They even had a slogan: "The Pack Will Be Back." Indeed, the Packers shut out the Bears in the season opener and held off the San Francisco 49ers to break out to a 2–0 start. And thanks to a dominating defense, the Packers were 5–2 at the halfway point.

But injuries again flared up and the Pack suffered a three-game losing streak in November during which they scored a total of 23 points. The Packers looked old and tired.

Starr missed the final four games of the season with a shoulder injury, and though his replacement, Don Horn, led Green Bay to three wins during that span, it was too little, too late. Green Bay finished 8–6 in 1969 and, for the second straight season, placed third in the NFL Central Division.

If it wasn't obvious before, it was crystal clear after that season: The Packers of Vince Lombardi had run their course.

Now what?

A fallen Starr: Age and injuries finally caught up with the Packers in 1969, as Bart Starr (15) showed in this game. The two-time defending Super Bowl champs tumbled to an 8–6 record in '69.

The glory days had come to an end, but Green Bay fans remained devoted to their team. No matter what happens on the field, Packer Backers are the most loyal fans in the NFL.

WE BACK OUR "PACK"

WISCONSIN LABEL CORP., ALGOMA 54201

The Packers on *Monday Night Football*

With the advent of the 1970s, change came to the very fabric of the NFL. Beginning in 1970, ABC-TV partnered with the NFL to televise games on Monday nights. It was a bold experiment, and no one really knew if the American TV-viewing public would take to football on a weeknight.

In their first appearance on Monday Night Football, *the Packers staged a late-game comeback to defeat the San Diego Chargers 22–20. Here, running back Travis Williams (23) carries the ball.*

Teams didn't like the concept at first because it disrupted their routines. But once they realized that they had the football spotlight to themselves for one night, they came around.

The Packers were tapped to play in the fourth *Monday Night Football* game in history when they traveled to San Diego to play the Chargers on October 12, 1970. The Packers led 19–6 going into the fourth quarter, thanks to two Bart Starr touchdown passes and two Dale Livingston field goals. But San Diego, one of the up-and-coming teams from the AFL, fought back to take

a 20–19 lead late in the game. Undaunted, Green Bay rebounded and won the game 22–20 on a 14-yard field goal kicked by Livingston. The victory moved the Packers to 3–1 for the season, but they'd manage only three more wins the rest of the way. For one night, though, the magic was back.

In the 1970s, Don Meredith, Howard Cosell, and Frank Gifford (left to right) were as much the stars of ABC's Monday Night Football *as the players on the field.*

Must-see TV

The Packers played their first *Monday Night Football* game on October 12, 1970, squeaking out a 22–20 victory over the San Diego Chargers. From 1970 through the 2008 season, the Packers appeared in 54 *Monday Night Football* games with an overall record of 27–27. The Pack's longest *MNF* winning streak—five games—took place between September 24, 2001, and September 29, 2003. Their longest *MNF* losing streak also lasted for five games—three games in 2005 and two in 2006. They also own the NFC's streak for the most consecutive seasons with an appearance on *Monday Night Football*—18 through the 2010 season.

A Little Devine Intervention

The Phil Bengtson experiment clearly didn't work. In three seasons, Vince Lombardi's handpicked successor suffered the fate of all too many coaches whose major flaw was that they weren't the guys they replaced.

But it was inevitable that the Packers would fall from grace, as the stars of the '60s got older and retired and the team failed to replenish its talent base in the draft. As a result, Bengtson's three teams were 20–21–1—not horrendous but certainly not up to previous standards. So, not surprisingly, Bengtson resigned after the 1970 season.

What followed was a schism within the Packers' organization over whom to pick next. The team's officials decided that they wanted to go into the college ranks to find a successful, well-known coach who could take the Packers in a new direction. Executive committee president Dominic Olejniczak set his sights on three top-flight college coaches—specifically, Penn State's Joe Paterno, Arizona State's hard-nosed Frank Kush, and Missouri's successful Dan Devine.

In the end, after a fractious meeting, a split executive committee decided to hire Devine, even though several committee members, including Packers legend Tony Canadeo, wanted Paterno (however, there was no guarantee that Paterno—who in 2009 broke a record for most years [44] as head coach at a single school—would have even accepted the job).

It was an inauspicious start to Devine's short, strange journey in Green Bay. He had never been a pro coach before but had built a strong reputation as a tactician and motivator in 16 seasons in the college ranks—three years at Arizona

Fans had high hopes when Dan Devine took over as head coach in 1971, but the Packers stumbled to a 25–27–4 record during his tenure.

State and 13 at Missouri, where he won two Big Eight titles and went to six bowl games.

But Devine—an Augusta, Wisconsin, native—did not get off on the right foot with his new squad. In his first meeting with the players, he showed highlights of his Missouri teams and, in a form of sacrilege, claimed that the famous "Packers Sweep," which had been immortalized by Lombardi, was actually *his* invention.

Coach Dan Devine confers with quarterbacks coach Bart Starr and their two QBs: Scott Hunter (left) and Jerry Tagge (right).

He also installed rules that may have worked well with college juniors but not NFL veterans. These included his insistence that every player keep his shoes shined and his pants pressed.

On September 19, 1971, Devine's career with the Packers began rather painfully against the New York Giants at Lambeau Field. Perhaps it was a sign of things to come when one of his own players plowed into him and broke his left leg as he stood on the sidelines in the fourth quarter. The Packers lost 42–40.

It didn't get much better the rest of the season, as the Packers stumbled through a 4–8–2 campaign. The lone highlight came in the next-to-last game of the season, when the Packers smacked the equally woeful Bears 31–10.

It looked bleak for the organization, especially when quarterback Bart Starr, the last real connection to the glory years, retired after the season.

The Packers were officially starting over.

THE "PACK" is Devine

"THE DEVINE ERA"

Back on Top...Briefly

For one lone season in the '70s, it all came together for the Green Bay Packers. Riding a ground attack led by John Brockington and MacArthur Lane and a defense that was reminiscent of the glory years, the 1972 Packers found themselves back on top of the National Football Conference's Central Division.

At halfback was Brockington, who had rushed for 1,105 yards as a rookie in 1971 and ran for another 1,027 yards in 1972. Added to the mix was the fullback Lane, an acquisition from the St. Louis Cardinals, who ran for another 821 yards and also caught a team-high 26 passes. And not to be forgotten was rookie kicker Chester Marcol, a talented import from Poland who kicked what is still a club-record 33 field goals. (Ryan Longwell tied the mark in 2000.)

Coach Dan Devine knew what he had and what he didn't have. Unfortunately, one of the things he didn't have was a trustworthy quarterback. Indeed, QB Scott Hunter completed just 86 passes and threw only six touchdown passes the entire season. And yet somehow the Packers still managed a 10–4 record.

Scott Hunter (16) hands the ball to John Brockington (42) in a 26–10 win over the Cleveland Browns on September 17, 1972. Brockington was a driving force on a Green Bay squad that went 10–4 and reached the playoffs in 1972.

In the first round of the playoffs, however, the Washington Redskins found the key to beating the Packers. Using an innovative six-man defensive front, the Redskins choked off Brockington and Lane's running, and Hunter was simply not gifted enough as a thrower to beat the Redskins' passing game.

Stubbornly, Devine refused to alter his game plan despite pleadings from Bart Starr, who, by that time, had assumed the role of Packers quarterbacks coach. In the end, the Packers fell 16–3; several players grumbled afterward that Green Bay was still the better team that season.

Nevertheless, after a five-year hiatus, many Packers fans believed that their team was back. But not for long.

A Draft Disaster

By 1973, it was clear that the Packers needed help at quarterback. Scott Hunter wasn't the answer, and the team's two other young signal-callers—Jim Del Gaizo and Jerry Tagge—didn't exactly inspire terror in opposing defenses, either.

As a result, the Packers fell back to 5–7–2 in 1973, which prompted Dan Devine to make a decision that even today is considered one of the biggest blunders in NFL history. Midway through the 1974 season, as Green Bay sat in a decent position with a 3–4 record, Devine inexplicably gave the Los Angeles Rams the

In 1974, in one of the worst trades in Packers—and NFL—history, Green Bay surrendered five future draft picks to the Rams for 34-year-old John Hadl.

Packers' first-, second-, and third-round draft choices in 1975 and the team's first- and third-round picks in '76 for 34-year-old quarterback John Hadl. The move all but signaled the end of Devine's tenure in Green Bay and crippled the Packers for years to come.

In a season and a half of work in Green Bay, Hadl threw only nine touchdown passes and an astounding 29 interceptions. And after posting a 6–8 record in 1974, Devine resigned to take over as head coach at Notre Dame.

A Starr to the Rescue

After four seasons, Dan Devine had worn out his welcome in Green Bay. One winning season in that time did not quell the frustration of fans who wanted a consistent winner back in Titletown. Indeed, there was plenty of anger directed toward Devine, and it led to one of the greatest urban myths in Packers history.

In 1974, as another season spun into oblivion, Devine did an interview with *Time* magazine in which he hinted that some irate Packers fans had shot his dog in front of his home. The story took on a life of its own, and the alleged shooting eventually turned into a torturous attack on the dog with—of all things—a pitch-fork. To this day, no one knows if the story is true, but it sure seemed newsworthy at the time.

After the 1974 season—and after he'd shattered the Packers' future with a disastrous trade for quarterback John Hadl—Devine resigned to become head coach at Notre Dame.

The door could not have closed on Devine any quicker as he exited, and on December 24, 1974, the Packers again turned to their glorious past when the executive committee hired Bart Starr to take over as head coach and general manager.

Starr was known as Vince Lombardi's "coach on the field" during his playing days, and the Packers' organization hoped that this experience would translate to success as an actual coach on the sidelines.

Starr had spent the '72 season as Devine's quarterbacks coach but left the following year to devote time to his automobile dealerships and to do some work as a TV analyst. But when the Packers called, Starr could not refuse, and though he'd never been a head coach of anything, anywhere, he accepted.

To some, it was a bold stroke; to others, it was a disaster waiting to happen. Even former teammate Bob Skoronski, a close friend, cautioned Starr not to take the job, telling him that he had nothing to gain from it.

But Starr felt the pull of responsibility. "I ask for your prayers and patience," he said in his first press conference as head coach of the Green Bay Packers. "We will earn everything else."

If only it were that simple.

In nine sometimes turbulent, often frustrating years, Starr managed just two winning campaigns—8–7–1 in 1978 and 5–3–1 during the strike-shortened 1982 season, when he led the Packers to the playoffs.

Starr compiled a 52–76–3 record and was fired after the 1983 season. To this day, he politely declines to talk about his coaching experience.

As a quarterback, Bart Starr did indeed live up to his name, but in his nine seasons as head coach of the Packers, he compiled a less-than-stellar 52–76–3 record.

FRESH START with Bart

Fans and the media alike trumpeted a return to glory as Bart Starr took over as head coach of the Green Bay Packers in 1975.

GREEN BAY PACKER

GOLDEN ANNIVERSARY YEAR

CURLY LAMBEAU

PHIL BENGTSON

★ 1919 ★ ★ ★ 1969 ★

SCHEDULE

				PACKERS	OPPONENTS
SEPT. 21	CHICAGO BEARS	at GREEN BAY	1:00 P.M.	17	0
SEPT. 28	SAN FRAN. 49'ers	at MILWAUKEE	1:00 P.M.	14	7
OCT. 5	MINN. VIKINGS	at MPLS.	1:30 P.M.	7	19
OCT. 12	DETROIT LIONS	at DETROIT	12:15 P.M.	28	17
OCT. 19	L.A. RAMS	at LOS ANGELES	3:00 P.M.	21	34
OCT. 26	ATLANTA FALCONS	at GREEN BAY	1:00 P.M.	28	10
NOV. 2	PITTSBURGH	at PITTSBURGH	12:15 P.M.	38	34
NOV. 9	BALTIMORE COLTS	at BALTIMORE	1:00 P.M.	6	14
NOV. 16	MINN. VIKINGS	at MILWAUKEE	1:00 P.M.	7	9
NOV. 23	DETROIT LIONS	at GREEN BAY	1:00 P.M.	10	16
NOV. 30	N. Y. GIANTS	at MILWAUKEE	3:00 P.M.	20	10
DEC. 7	CLEVE. BROWNS	at CLEVELAND	12:30 P.M.	7	20
DEC. 14	CHICAGO BEARS	at CHICAGO	1:00 P.M.	28	27
DEC. 21	ST. LOUIS	at GREEN BAY	1:00 P.M.	45	28

This schedule shows that the Packers went 8-6 in 1969 to mark their 50th anniversary as a professional football team. Although they finished in a respectable third place, it was nothing compared to the glory years under Curly Lambeau and Vince Lombardi.

GREEN BAY PRESS-GAZETTE
VOLUME LVI, No. 67   48 PAGES   GREEN BAY, WIS., THURSDAY EVENING, SEPTEMBER 3, 1970   PRICE 15¢

Coaching Great Succumbs to Cancer
Legendary Lombardi Dies

Vince Lombardi ... As Packer Coach

The Green Bay Years

Vince Built a Dynasty, Legend Here

Features on Vince Lombardi

It was a sad day for Green Bay fans and anyone who followed football, when legendary coach Vince Lombardi died on September 3, 1970. The front page of the *Press-Gazette* reminisced about his days with the Packers.

GO PACK GO!
GO ALL THE WAY!

GREEN BAY AREA CHAMBER OF COMMERCE SPORTS COMMITTEE

Packers memorabilia from the early 1970s, like this "Go Pack Go" sticker, show that fans were eager to continue the winning tradition that was so prevalent under Vince Lombardi.

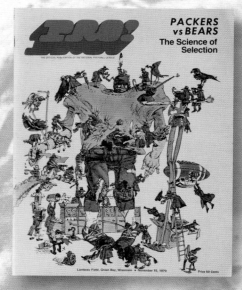

PACKERS vs BEARS
The Science of Selection

Tiny NFL mascots futilely try to take down a gigantic Packer on the cover of this game program from November 15, 1970. The Bears took their best shot that day, but the Pack squeaked past them 20-19.

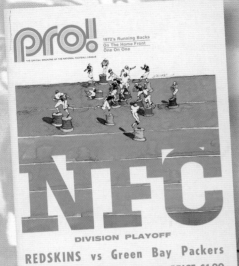

PACKERS vs Green Bay Packers

DIVISION PLAYOFF
REDSKINS vs Green Bay Packers
DECEMBER 24, 1972   PRICE $1.00

The Packers faced the Redskins in the 1972 division playoffs. It would be a blue Christmas for the Packers as the Redskins knocked them off by a score of 16-3.

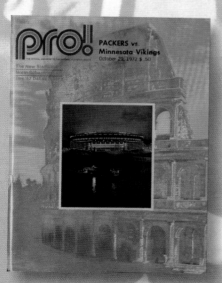

On October 29, 1972, the Vikes scored 17 unanswered points in the fourth quarter to put the Packers away 27-13.

GREEN BAY PACKERS
1972 YEAR BOOK

After winning a Rookie of the Year Award in 1971, John Brockington (42) made the cover of the Packers' 1972 yearbook. That year, he rushed for 1,027 yards and helped lead the Packers to the playoffs.

The 1972 Packers faced a tough schedule, but stars such as MacArthur Lane, John Brockington, Willie Buchanon, Dave Hanner, and Chester Marcol led them to a 10-4 record and a first-place finish.

1972 GREEN BAY PACKER SQUAD

TOP ROW: 87 Al Roche, 67 Malcolm Snider, 10 Frank Patrick, 64 Kevin Hunt, 73 Vern Vanoy, 83 Clarence Williams, 77 Bill Hayhoe, 65 Keith Wortman, 75 Dave Pureifory, 13 Chester Marcol, 23 Bob Hudson, 46 Leland Glass, 51 Larry Hefner, 50 Jim Carter.
SECOND ROW FROM TOP: 88 Len Garrett, 71 Francis Peay, 81 Rich McGeorge, 56 Tommy Joe Crutcher, 84 Carroll Dale, 16 Scott Hunter, 21 Charlie Hall, 42 John Brockington, 28 Willie Buchanon, 30 Larry Krause, 76 Mike McCoy, 47 Dave Davis, 22 John Staggers, 37 Ike Thomas.
THIRD ROW FROM TOP (standing): Dominic Gentile (Trainer), 17 Jerry Tagge, 20 Don Widby, 78 Bob Brown, 36 MacArthur Lane, Rollie Dotsch, Red Cochran, Bart Starr, Dan Devine, Dave Hanner, John Polonchek, Don Doll, 33 Charlie Pittman, 11 Charlie Napper, 44 Bob Kroll, Dad Braisher (Equipment Mgr.), Bob Noel (Asst. Equipment Mgr.).
BOTTOM ROW: 57 Ken Bowman, 58 Cal Withrow, 62 Bill Lueck, 72 Dick Himes, 39 Jim Hill, 66 Ray Nitschke, 89 Dave Robinson, 68 Dale Gillingham, 29 Al Matthews, 48 Ken Ellis, 31 Perry Williams, 40 Dave Kopay, 53 Fred Carr.
(not present when picture taken: Coaches Burt Gustafson and Hank Kuhlmann and player #41 Paul Gibson)

GREEN BAY PACKERS
1972 FOOTBALL SCHEDULE
all times local, daylight or standard

PRE-SEASON GAMES
Sat., Aug. 5 . . . . . Cincinnati Bengals at Green Bay 8 p.m.
Sat., Aug. 12 . . . . Miami Dolphins at Miami 8 p.m.
Sat., Aug. 19 . . . . . Houston Oilers at Houston 8 p.m.
Sun., Aug. 27 . . . . Chicago Bears at Milw. 8 p.m.
Sept. 2 . . . St. Louis Card. at Green Bay 8 p.m.
Sat., Sept. 9 . . . . Kansas City Chiefs at Milw. 8 p.m.

LEAGUE GAMES
Sun., Sept. 17 . . . . . . Cleveland Browns at Clev. 1 p.m.
Sun., Sept. 24 . . Oakland Raiders at Green Bay 1 p.m.
Sun., Oct. 1 . . . . Dallas Cowboys at Milw. 1 p.m.
Sun., Oct. 8 . . . . . Chicago Bears at Green Bay 1 p.m.
Mon., Oct. 16 . . . . . . Detroit Lions at Detroit 8 p.m.
Sun., Oct. 22 . . . . Atlanta Falcons at Milw. 1 p.m.
Sun., Oct. 29 . . Minnesota Vikings at Green Bay 1 p.m.
Sun., Nov. 5 . . . San Francisco 49'ers at Milw. 1 p.m.
Sun., Nov. 12 . . . . . Chicago Bears at Chicago 1 p.m.
Sun., Nov. 19 . . . Houston Oilers at Houston 1 p.m.
Sun., Nov. 26 . . Washington Redskins at Wash. 1 p.m.
Sun., Dec. 3 . . . . . Detroit Lions at Green Bay 1 p.m.
Sun., Dec. 10 . . . Minnesota Vikings at Minn. 1 p.m.
Sun., Dec. 17 . . . . New Orleans Saints at N.O. 1 p.m.

THE STUEBE CO.

Passing Fancy

It is perhaps one of the great ironies of Packers history that a player who was involved in one of the worst trades in franchise history would also be involved in one of the team's best.

By 1976, the Packers' quarterback situation was intolerable, and Bart Starr knew that despite what the Packers had given up to get him, John Hadl wasn't the answer. So a week before the 1976 NFL draft, Starr packaged Hadl, defensive back Ken Ellis, a fourth-round pick in the following week's draft, and a third-rounder in the 1977 draft, and sent them to the Houston Oilers for quarterback Lynn Dickey.

Although his career was marked by injury and featured more losses than wins, Dickey became the face of a Green Bay Packers offense that evolved into one of the most entertaining units in the NFL in the early 1980s.

Lynn Dickey (12) looks to throw in a December 5, 1982 game against the Buffalo Bills. The quarterback's best season came the following year when he threw for a league-best 4,458 yards and 32 touchdowns.

A Bad Break

Oh, what might have been if only Bart Starr had taken Lynn Dickey out of a game that the Packers had no hope of winning.

Instead, on the last play of the Packers' November 13, 1977, game against the Los Angeles Rams—a game that Green Bay was losing 24–6—Dickey was tackled so hard that his left leg was shattered.

The result was a nearly two-year ordeal that almost cost Dickey his career and certainly cost him bigger and better statistics. The injury was so severe that he missed the entire '78 season as he underwent several operations, including the insertion of a metal rod in his leg.

On October 28, 1979, against the Miami Dolphins, Dickey finally returned in relief of starter David Whitehurst. Dickey started three games later that season and threw five touchdown passes; he reclaimed his starting spot in 1980.

Dickey was the Packers' first true gunslinger long before Brett Favre adopted the role. He threw for 300 or more yards 15 times in his career, and his 4,458 passing yards during the 1983 season remains a club record.

Over the course of his Packers career (1976–85), Dickey threw for 21,369 yards and 133 touchdowns; both marks rank third in team history behind Favre and Starr.

But injuries dogged Dickey his entire career, including in 1984 as he was coming to the end of another excellent season in which he threw for 3,195 yards and 25 touchdowns in 15 games. While working out prior to the Packers' December 9 game against the Bears, he seriously injured his neck. He retired after the '85 season.

Dickey considered coaching but knew that he couldn't give the commitment that the job required, so he made a second career for himself in the automobile warranty business in Kansas City. He was inducted into the Packers Hall of Fame in 1992.

A Close Call: The '78 Packers

No one denied that the hiring of Bart Starr was a gamble. He had never been a head coach before, but apparently, the people who mattered in the Packers' organization thought it was a risk worth taking.

Nevertheless, in his first three seasons, Starr proved the naysayers absolutely correct. From 1975 to 1977, the Packers were a miserable 13–29, and, again, there were rumblings about changing the man calling the shots.

But then, as has been known to happen from time to time in pro sports, a season that left players and fans alike scratching their heads in curiosity and disbelief arose from out of nowhere.

There was no reason to believe that the 1978 Packers would be any different from the '77 team that had finished a pallid 4–10. Indeed, it seemed that the team would be far worse without quarterback Lynn Dickey, who would miss the entire '78 season recovering from a severely broken leg. David Whitehurst, an unknown eighth-round draft pick in '77, filled in at QB.

But something clicked for the Packers that season. Bolstered by terrific drafts in 1977 and '78, these young Packers had talent and swagger and they didn't care about the mediocrity of the recent past.

The '78 Packers were led by defensive ends Mike Butler and Ezra Johnson, who were first-round picks in 1977, and wide receiver James Lofton, a first-round pick from Stanford in 1978. In those two drafts, the Packers found 11 eventual starters.

On offense, Lofton led the Pack with 46 receptions and six touchdowns, while Terdell Middleton ran for 1,116 yards and 11 touchdowns. Whitehurst, who did his best to manage games, threw for 2,093 yards and ten touchdowns.

The Packers opened the season by winning six of their first seven games before losing six of their last nine, including a costly 21–7 decision to the Minnesota Vikings in October that would ultimately cost Green Bay a division title. Although the Packers and Vikings finished with identical 8–7–1 records, Minnesota claimed the Central Division title by virtue of the team's victory over Green Bay.

The Packers also missed out on a wild-card playoff berth by a half game; the Atlanta Falcons secured that spot with a 9–7 record. But two things happened as a result of the team's unexpected success: Questions about Starr's future stopped—at least for the moment—and Packers fans acquired a renewed hope in their franchise.

James Lofton set the NFL on fire during his rookie season, when he caught 46 passes, averaged nearly 18 yards per catch, and scored six touchdowns. In nine seasons with Green Bay, Lofton caught 530 passes.

Going Nowhere...Fast

If the 1978 season was a pleasant, unexpected surprise for the Green Bay Packers, the years that followed were as forgettable—and downright embarrassing—as any in the history of the franchise.

Indeed, even Bart Starr admitted years later that the '78 team, which just barely missed a playoff spot and sparked a belief that better days were ahead, wasn't as good as it appeared.

That assessment became abundantly clear in 1979, when the Packers started out 1–3 and ultimately sputtered to a 5–11 record, their eighth losing season of the decade. Even worse, it looked as though Starr was losing control of his team.

After a key James Lofton fumble in a loss to the New York Jets on November 4, boos rained down from the Lambeau Field crowd, which prompted Lofton to respond with an obscene gesture that was directed at the stands. When asked about the incident after the game, Lofton grumbled, "[The fans] can shove it as far as I'm concerned."

A new decade did not solve the problem. Green Bay's first-round draft pick in 1980, Penn State defensive tackle Bruce Clark, refused to sign with the Packers and instead took a more lucrative deal with the Toronto Argonauts of the Canadian Football League. It was a mortifying slap in the face to both the NFL and the Packers' organization.

The Packers responded with a winless preseason in which they scored just 17 points in five games. The highlight (or lowlight) of the preseason came during a 38–0 loss to the Broncos, when defensive end Ezra Johnson was seen munching a hot dog on the sidelines.

All of this turmoil culminated in a 5–10–1 regular season that saw the Packers lose their final four games by a combined score of 127–30, including a disastrous 61–7 thrashing at the hands of their bitter rival, the Chicago Bears.

If the Packers hadn't hit rock bottom, they could certainly touch it with their tippy toes.

A Support System

Fans were angry, embarrassed, and confused by what had happened to their beloved Packers. But through it all, and maybe despite it all, they stayed loyal. Nothing demonstrated this more than "Packer Support Sunday," which took place prior to the team's November 1, 1981, game against the Seattle Seahawks.

Heading into the matchup, the Packers were still spinning their wheels—they had lost three straight and sat at 2–6 for the season. Nevertheless, thousands of fans turned out at Lambeau Field to show their support and love for a team that had done little to earn it in recent years.

Energized by the demonstration, the Packers beat the Seahawks 34–24 and went on to win five of their last seven games. In fact, the Pack had made such a miraculous comeback that they could have secured a playoff spot with a season-ending win over the New York Jets.

But a miracle was not in the cards, as the Packers fell to the Jets 28–3.

In the early 1980s, the Packers offense could score on anyone. Unfortunately, the defense, as shown in this December 20, 1981, game against the New York Jets, was often a disaster.

A Striking Season

After winning six of the last eight games of the 1981 season, the Packers—and their fans—were again teased by the hope that better days were on the horizon.

As the 1982 season dawned, every team knew that a potentially crippling players strike loomed, which could alter the season dramatically. But until it happened, the Packers knew that there was only one thing to do: Play and let the chips fall where they may.

The season opener was a stunner for the Packers, as they trailed the Los Angeles Rams 23–0 at halftime. But a second-half surge, sparked by three Lynn Dickey touchdown passes, led to the biggest rally in team history and a confidence-boosting 35–23 win. They followed it up with a 27–19 victory over the New York Giants on *Monday Night Football*.

Hours later, the strike hit. It lasted 57 days and cost Green Bay seven games. But when the season resumed on November 21, the Pack picked up where they left off, beating the Minnesota Vikings 26–7.

Thanks to the strike-reduced schedule that included the cancellation of two games against the Chicago Bears as well as matchups against the powerful Tampa Bay Buccaneers and Miami Dolphins, the

James Lofton hauls in a touchdown pass against the Cowboys during an NFC playoff game in Texas on January 16, 1983.

Packers posted a 5–3–1 record. And because of the expanded eight-team playoff tournament, the Packers also earned their first postseason appearance since 1972.

Indeed, when they opened the playoffs against the St. Louis Cardinals, it was the first time that Green Bay had hosted a playoff game since the "Ice Bowl" in 1967.

In front of a raucous sell-out crowd at Lambeau Field, the Packers unloaded on the unsuspecting Cardinals, jumping out to a 28–9 halftime lead and coasting to a 41–16 win. Lynn Dickey threw for 260 yards and four touchdowns, including two to wide receiver John Jefferson, who set a team postseason record with 148 receiving yards on six receptions.

The win over the Cardinals set up a second-round meeting against the Dallas Cowboys in Texas. It was a game that could have shown the rest of the NFL that the Packers really had returned from the wasteland.

Unfortunately, the Packers fell behind the Cowboys 20–7 by halftime, and despite rolling up 466 total yards, they could not overcome the experienced, playoff-tested Cowboys. Dickey completed 19 of 36 passes for 332 yards, but he also threw three interceptions, one of which was returned for a touchdown by Dennis Thurman. The Packers fell 37–26.

But even in defeat, the Packers could see the future. This was a team with a potent offense, and if they could just put the pieces together on defense, maybe the Pack really could come back.

Dennis Thurman of Dallas celebrates his touchdown after intercepting a Lynn Dickey pass during the NFC playoffs in January 1983. The Packers played them tough, but the Cowboys prevailed 37–26.

The Packers and their ever-loyal fans went through some tough times in the '70s and '80s, but the love affair continued, as this button shows.

The Packers and their fans were pleased with a first-place finish under Dan Devine in 1972, but losing seasons during the rest of his tenure did not live up to post-Lombardi expectations.

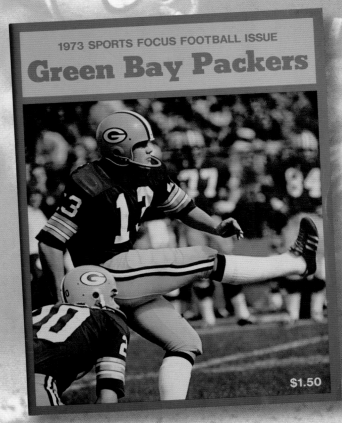

Kicker Chester Marcol's 33 field goals in 1972 set a record for rookies and garnered him Rookie of the Year honors. He also earned a spot on the cover of the Packers' 1973 yearbook.

By the 1970s, the Packers had racked up 11 NFL championships, making the tiny Wisconsin town of Green Bay deserving of the nickname "Titletown, U.S.A."

The cover of this program featured the Pro Football Hall of Fame's Class of '77, which included Packers greats Bart Starr (top right) and Forrest Gregg (bottom left).

When Bart Starr took over as head coach in 1975, the Packers and their followers were hopeful that his heroics on the field would carry over to the sidelines.

By the late 1970s, Packers paraphernalia, like this pennant and button, were starting to look more modern, except for the single-bar face mask, which was on its way out of style.

Lofty Ambitions

James Lofton soared into Green Bay as a first-round draft pick in 1978. He was the kind of deep threat as a receiver that the Packers hadn't really had since the days of Don Hutson.

Lofton played 16 seasons in the NFL—retiring after the 1993 season—but he is still most identified for his nine seasons with the Packers (1978–86), during which he caught 530 passes for 9,656 yards, which remains a club record. He also had 32 games in which he gained 100 or more receiving yards, which is also a club record. And in 1983 and '84, he led the league in yards per catch, averaging a remarkable 22.4 and 22 yards, respectively.

Despite his "lofty" statistics, Lofton and Green Bay battled through a love-hate relationship. Once, after a loss to the Vikings, he got into a locker room argument with head coach Bart Starr. Later that season, after being booed for a fumble, Lofton made

Oh, What a Night!

At Lambeau Field, on October 17, 1983, the Packers and the defending Super Bowl champion Washington Redskins engaged in an offensive showdown for the ages. The Packers had one of the NFL's best offenses—and one of the league's worst defenses—and the Redskins may have come in a little overconfident.

The result was a wild offensive show in which the two teams combined for 95 points (still a *Monday Night Football* record) and 1,025 total yards. Quarterback Lynn Dickey led the way, throwing for 387 yards and three touchdowns. "We knew no one could really stop us," he said.

Trouble was, the Packers couldn't stop anybody either, and Redskins quarterback Joe Theismann threw for 398 yards of his own. In the end, the Packers prevailed 48–47 after Redskins kicker Mark Moseley missed a 39-yard field goal in the final seconds.

In what has become a Monday Night Football legend, the Packers beat the Redskins 48–47.

James Lofton (80) helped revolutionize the Packers' passing game and gave Green Bay one of the most feared offensive units in the early 1980s.

an obscene gesture at the Lambeau Field crowd. Then, late in the '86 season, he was charged with second-degree sexual assault for an incident at a Milwaukee hotel; he was cleared of those charges, but the Packers still decided to cut ties with their record-setting receiver. After the 1986 season, Lofton was traded to the Los Angeles Raiders for third- and fourth-round draft picks.

Lofton spent two years with the Raiders (1987–88) and four seasons with the Buffalo Bills (1989–92), and finished up in 1993 with the Rams and Eagles. He retired with 764 receptions for 14,004 yards—an average of 18.3 yards per catch, which is a remarkable number even today.

Lofton was inducted into the Packers Hall of Fame in 1999 and the Pro Football Hall of Fame in 2003.

Bad Times and Bad Boys

The Green Bay Packers gave Bart Starr nine seasons to turn the team around, and in the NFL, that's an eternity. But after Green Bay finished the 1983 season 8–8 and missed out on a playoff berth thanks to a heartbreaking 23–21 last-minute loss to the Bears, enough was enough. Starr was fired the next day.

The franchise's focus fell on another Packers legend, Forrest Gregg, the Hall of Fame guard and tackle who was a year removed from having coached the Cincinnati Bengals to Super Bowl XVI (a loss to the San Francisco 49ers). He had also spent three seasons as head coach of the Cleveland Browns (1975–77).

Gregg jumped at the opportunity to take over his old team, and he instilled in his troops an attitude that was the polar opposite to that of the good-natured Starr. Gregg wanted tough, hard-nosed players who weren't afraid to let opponents know that they wouldn't take anything from anyone. And there were times when Gregg's Packers went too far in that regard.

Indeed, during Gregg's tenure as head coach, from 1984 to 1987, the Packers developed a reputation as the NFL's bad boys. They were known for cheap shots and late hits, especially against the Chicago Bears. Although the rivalry had cooled in recent years, it flared back up in 1985, when the Bears embarrassed the Pack in a Monday night game by allowing defensive tackle William "The Refrigerator" Perry to score a touchdown during a 23–7 Chicago win. The next season, the Packers vowed revenge.

Forrest Gregg replaced Bart Starr as head coach in 1984, but he didn't have any more luck on the sidelines than his former teammate. Gregg's teams went 25–37–1 in four seasons.

Packers defensive end Charles Martin came into a 1986 game at Soldier Field with a towel listing the numbers of five Bears that he wanted to take down. He got one—quarterback Jim McMahon, whom he body-slammed to the ground after an interception. Later in that same game, Packers cornerback Ken Stills delivered a late hit on Bears fullback Matt Suhey. And so it went.

Linebacker Brian Noble, the Packers' fifth-round draft pick in 1985, was so appalled by what he saw that he apologized to Bears coach Mike Ditka after the game.

As Suhey was leaving the Bears' locker room, he ran across Packers executive Bob Harlan. Suhey said simply, "Bob, this has to stop."

In his four seasons with the Packers, Gregg had no more success than Starr, delivering a 25–37–1 record. After the '87 season, Gregg accepted an offer to become head coach at his alma mater, Southern Methodist University, which was trying to re-establish a football program after the NCAA had closed it down for two years due to repeated, grievous recruiting violations.

To Gregg, reviving a crippled college program seemed like a better option than coaching the Packers. And maybe it was.

FORREST FIRE '84

With an 8–8 finish in '84, Forrest Gregg didn't exactly ignite the Packers quite as much as fans had hoped.

It was a low point in the storied Packers–Bears rivalry. In a Monday night contest in 1985, defensive tackle William "The Refrigerator" Perry (72) scored a touchdown for the Bears, who embarrassed the Pack 23–7.

103

Stars of the Era

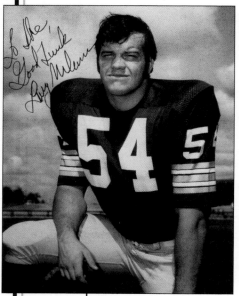

Two-time Pro Bowler Larry McCarren played his entire career (12 seasons) with the Green Bay Packers.

Larry McCarren's nickname said it all—"Rock." One of the great overachievers in team history, this University of Illinois product was a 12th-round draft pick in 1973. He took over at center in 1974 and didn't leave the lineup for the next 11 years.

Although McCarren was an All-Pro in 1982 and a Pro Bowler in '82 and '83, he still labored in relative obscurity. But his toughness was legendary. In 1980, McCarren was recovering from hernia surgery as the season began. Coach Bart Starr decided to start McCarren in the season opener to keep his streak of consecutive games played intact but planned to take him out after one play. McCarren waved off his replacement and played the entire game. He also played most of the season with a broken hand.

McCarren played in 162 consecutive games over 12 seasons before a pinched nerve in his neck forced him to sit out late in the 1984 season. He tried to come back in 1985, but the injury persisted, and he retired. He was inducted into the Packers Hall of Fame in 1992.

John Brockington was the Packers' top draft choice in 1971. As a member of Woody Hayes's 1968 Ohio State Buckeyes, who went undefeated and won a national championship, Brockington wasted no time making his presence felt in a Packers uniform. During his rookie season, he rushed for 1,105 yards, which garnered him All-Pro and Pro Bowl honors and helped him secure the 1971 NFL Offensive Rookie of the Year Award.

In 1972, Brockington teamed up with fullback MacArthur Lane to give the Packers a devastating running attack, which led

Green Bay to a 10–4 record and a spot in the NFC playoffs. That season, Brockington rushed for 1,027 yards and followed it with 1,144 yards in '73, making him the first back in NFL history to rush for more than 1,000 yards in each of his first three seasons.

But wear and tear soon caught up with Brockington, and he never again reached the 1,000-yard plateau. He was released by the Packers one game into the 1977 season. He finished out the '77 season with the Kansas City Chiefs before retiring. Brockington ended his Packers career with 5,024 rushing yards and was inducted into the Packers Hall of Fame in 1984.

Sometimes it's all about being in the right place at the right time. Although **Paul Coffman** was a star tight end at Kansas State, he went undrafted in 1978. But when the Packers needed a tight end to fill out the roster, assistant coach John Meyer thought of Coffman, who had worked out for him that spring.

By the beginning of the 1979 season, Coffman was Green Bay's starting tight end. He played for the Packers through 1985 and was a part of two winning teams (1978 and 1982). Along with wide

Above: *John Brockington rushed for 1,000-plus yards in each of his first three seasons.*
Below: *Paul Coffman still holds several Packers records.*

receivers James Lofton and John Jefferson and quarterback Lynn Dickey, he was an integral part of the prolific Packers offense that dominated the NFL in the early 1980s.

Coffman caught 322 passes, averaged 13 yards per catch, and scored 39 touchdowns during his time with the Packers—these all remain team records for Packers tight ends. After leaving Green Bay as a free agent in 1985, he played two seasons for the Kansas City Chiefs and one for the Minnesota Vikings before retiring after the 1988 season.

Coffman was an All-Pro in 1984, a Pro Bowler from 1982 to 1984, and was inducted into the Packers Hall of Fame in 1994.

Willie Buchanon saved his best season with the Packers for last. He was a first-round draft pick for Green Bay in 1972, but by 1978, the flashy cornerback had already decided to opt out of his contract and see what the open market could provide. Then, on September 24, 1978, in front of 300 friends and family, Buchanon intercepted four passes, returning one for a touchdown in Green Bay's 24–3 win over the San Diego Chargers.

In 1972, Willie Buchanon intercepted four passes and recovered three fumbles, earning him Defensive Rookie of the Year honors.

Buchanon, the NFC's Defensive Rookie of the Year in 1972, did indeed leave Green Bay after the '78 season. He signed with his hometown Chargers, with whom he played four seasons. In his seven seasons with the Packers, Buchanon intercepted 21 passes and was a three-time Pro Bowler (1973, '74, and '78). He was inducted into the Packers Hall of Fame in 1993.

In 1965, 15-year-old Czeslaw Boleslaw **"Chester" Marcol** came to America from Opole, Poland. He spoke no English and knew nothing of the American game of football. But he learned quickly.

Marcol began kicking footballs at tiny Imlay City High in Michigan, became a four-time NAIA All-American at nearby Hillsdale College, and in 1972, was the second-round draft choice of the Packers.

As a rookie in 1972, he made 33 of 48 field goals, by far a Packers record at that stage, and led the NFL in scoring with 128 points. Marcol was named NFL Rookie of the Year that season and was selected as an All-Pro and a Pro Bowler in both 1972 and 1974. He played nine seasons with the Packers, and his mark of 120 field goals still ranks third in team history. He was inducted into the Packers Hall of Fame in 1987.

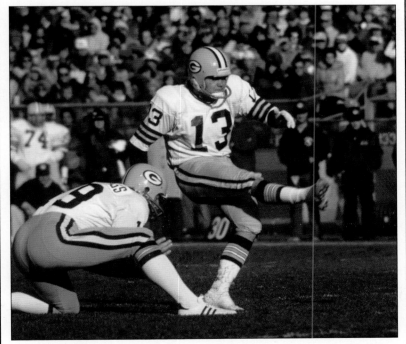

Chester Marcol (13), the Packers' first soccer-style kicker, twice led the league in scoring (1972 and '74). With 521 career points as a Packer, he was also the team's leading scorer in six of his eight-plus seasons in Green Bay.

A Suite Addition

When it was built in 1957, City Stadium seated 32,150 fans, and it seemed perfectly adequate for the times. But the team's popularity outdated the stadium almost as soon as it was finished, and by 1961, more than 6,500 seats had been added to the structure. Two years after that, another 3,600 seats were added, and in 1965, an additional 8,500 were installed, bringing capacity of the renamed Lambeau Field to 50,852.

This aerial view shows venerable Lambeau Field in 2003, after the completion of a $295 million renovation project.

By 1970, the team had added another 5,411 seats and enclosed the entire stadium in the classic bowl shape. But by 1985, a new phenomenon was evolving around the NFL and in pro sports in general: the concept of enclosed luxury boxes that could comfortably seat dozens of fans. Of course, these enclosed seats would cost more, but they would also provide special frills for those who could afford them.

The Packers made their first foray into the world of luxury boxes in 1985 by building 72 private suites that could hold another 663 spectators. This raised the capacity of Lambeau Field to 56,926, and also added to the team's revenues. Five years later, Lambeau Field's capacity jumped to 59,543 with the addition of luxury suites around the top rim of the stadium. By 1995, 1,300 more seats completely ringed the facility.

By 2001, as part of a $295 million renovation, more luxury boxes were added to swell the stadium's capacity to 65,290, and the next year, even more seats were added to the bowl, which increased Lambeau Field's capacity to 72,928.

Full House

Capacity of City Stadium/
Lambeau Field over the years:

Year	Capacity
1957:	32,150
1961:	38,669
1963:	42,327
1965:	50,852
1970:	56,263
1985:	56,926
1990:	59,543
1995:	60,890
2001:	65,290
2002:	72,928

In recent years, luxury boxes and suites have been added to Lambeau Field. They've helped to increase the team's revenue by millions of dollars.

It Was Snow Contest

Snow, freezing temperatures, and Green Bay just seem to go together. Indeed, there's an impression that by the time November rolls around, playing in Green Bay means playing in weather that's reminiscent of Siberia.

In truth, while opponents can usually count on the weather being cold late in the season, snowstorms during Packers home games have been relatively rare. But on December 1, 1985, a major Wisconsin snowstorm rolled into Green Bay as the Packers prepared to host the Tampa Bay Buccaneers.

The white stuff began falling overnight, and by morning, a foot of snow had already blanketed the area . . . with more on the way. But neither that nor the additional five inches that fell during the game, which has since been dubbed the "Snow Bowl," could deter the faithful crowd of 19,856, many who arrived on snowmobiles.

Packers receiver Preston Dennard couldn't even access the main road from his home to get to the game until 20 or so neighbors broke out their shovels and cleared a path. Meanwhile, the Buccaneers saw the weather they were facing and immediately wished that they could get back on their plane and go home.

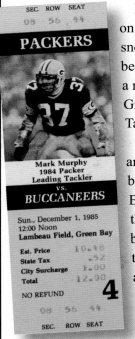

Fewer than 20,000 Packer Backers braved the elements for the "Snow Bowl" on December 1, 1985.

Not surprisingly, the Packers dominated the game, rolling up 512 total yards of offense and 31 first downs; the Bucs managed just 65 total yards and five first downs. Eddie Lee Ivery ran for 109 yards on 13 carries, and Gerry Ellis added another 101 yards on the ground as the Packers piled up 232 rushing yards. Amazingly, quarterback Lynn Dickey threw for 299 yards in the blustery blizzard conditions.

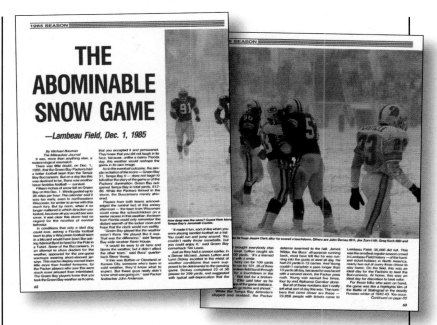

This article from the Packers' 1986 yearbook reminisces about the "Snow Bowl." Players were ankle-deep in the white stuff as the Pack blanked the Bucs 21–0.

In what was only his second NFL start, Bucs quarterback—and future Hall of Famer—Steve Young was sacked five times, including four takedowns by Packers defensive end Alphonso Carreker. To make matters worse for the visitors from sunny Florida, the Buccaneers were wearing their white road jerseys, which made it nearly impossible for fans and the media—and perhaps even fellow teammates—to see them, since they blended into the snow-covered field. And after every play, the Lambeau Field grounds crew was sent out to sweep the yard lines so the players knew where they were going.

Despite their dominance, the Packers committed four turnovers (two fumbles, two interceptions) compared to just one interception thrown by Tampa Bay. But the Packers still coasted to an easy 21–0 victory.

It was the true definition of a home-field advantage.

Cheeseheads

W hat began as an insult ended up an industry. In 1987, 27-year-old Milwaukee native Ralph Bruno watched as Chicago White Sox fans derided Milwaukee Brewers fans by calling them "Cheeseheads." Those Sox fans must have thought it was just about the worst thing you could say to someone who called Wisconsin home.

But Bruno didn't see it that way. "Personally, I like cheese a lot," he told the *Milwaukee Journal Sentinel* in 2005. "I decided to make a cheesehead so they'd know it's not a bad thing."

So Bruno took a piece of foam from a couch he was reupholstering, fashioned it into the shape of a cheese wedge, and wore it on his head to a Brewers game. It was an instant sensation.

Since 1987, cheesehead hats have taken the Dairy State by storm. Now cheesehead products come in many forms.

Later in 1987, Bruno formed Foamation Co. in St. Francis, Wisconsin, to manufacture the headwear, and these days, the ubiquitous cheeseheads can be found just about everywhere in the Dairy State. "People were amazed by something so silly," Bruno told the *Milwaukee Journal Sentinel*.

At first, cheeseheads were associated with the Brewers and were sold only at Milwaukee County Stadium. But they were soon replaced with cheese baseball caps after Brewers owner Bud Selig complained that the wedge-shape foam obstructed views.

The cheesehead phenomenon exploded among Packers fans

A cheesehead hat is a standard part of the uniform for many Packers fans.

during the mid-1990s, when the Packers were once again among the elite teams in the NFL. And it eventually became more than just cheesehead hats—Bruno's company now makes cheese ties, cheese earrings, cheese coasters, and many other foam cheese products.

A cheesehead chapeau reportedly even saved the life of Frank Emmert, Jr., of Superior, Wisconsin. In 1995, Emmert was returning home from watching a Packers game when the Cessna in which he was flying developed engine trouble. As the plane went down, Emmert used his cheesehead as a pillow to cushion the blow. Although he suffered several injuries, it could have been a lot worse had it not been for his quick thinking—and his cheesehead!

Cheeseheads hold a special place in the hearts of many Packers fans, though admittedly, many feel that the whole idea is a bad stereotype that Wisconsinites shouldn't perpetuate.

But Bruno disagrees. "I'm still here today doing it because I believe it's not a bad thing to be from Wisconsin," he said.

Doing the Lindy

When Forrest Gregg resigned as Green Bay's head coach on January 15, 1988, the Packers already had a plan in place: They would abandon the former-Packers-star-as-head-coach routine in favor of hiring the best coach available. They settled immediately on Michigan State's George Perles, who had just led the Spartans to a Rose Bowl victory.

Talks with Perles seemed to go smoothly, and the announcement of his hiring was imminent when the coach stunned the Packers by backing out. Green Bay scrambled to recover and went to their No. 2 choice, Lindy Infante, who had made a name for himself as the Cleveland Browns' offensive coordinator.

Infante's first season as Packers head coach was plagued, most notably, by kicking problems. Incredibly, he went through four kickers on the way to a 4–12 season.

But Infante caught lightning in a bottle in 1989. With Don Majkowski at quarterback, the Packers were one of the NFL's great stories that year, winning four games in the last minute and a half and posting a 10–6 record that left them just shy of the playoffs.

Lindy Infante became head coach of the Packers in 1988 after Michigan State coach George Perles accepted the job but backed out at the last minute.

Infante was named NFL Coach of the Year, and Packers fans were thrilled. So, too, was the front office, which gave Infante a two-year contract extension through 1994. And in a fan poll conducted by the *Milwaukee Journal* during the off-season, Infante was named the Packers' best coach of all time—even outdistancing fellows named Lombardi and Lambeau!

But 1990 was a completely different story. Team unity was shattered when Majkowski refused to sign a contract until just before the start of the regular season, and after a decent 6–5 start, the Packers lost their final five games. And in 1991, the Packers collapsed to 4–12.

But changes were coming…again. Ron Wolf, who had just assumed control as general manager, fired Infante the day after the 1991 season came to a close.

Grilled Braatz

Tom Braatz spent 1987 to 1991 as the Packers' executive vice president of football operations, a newly created position that was designed to take some of the pressure, and responsibility, away from the head coach.

During those years, Braatz was responsible for the trade of James Lofton and oversaw four drafts that produced quality players like Don Majkowski, Sterling Sharpe, Bryce Paup, LeRoy Butler, and Chris Jacke. However, Braatz also made the decision that Tony Mandarich was a better player than either Barry Sanders or Deion Sanders. And his last draft, in April 1991, may go down as the worst in team history, as none of the 14 players selected really amounted to anything.

So when team president Bob Harlan gave Ron Wolf complete control of all football decisions in late 1991, Braatz was no longer needed. He left to become the Miami Dolphins' general manager in 1992, where he remained until he retired in 2003.

The Majik Man

From 1988 to 1990, Don Majkowski was the biggest thing in Wisconsin since sliced cheese. He was the swaggering, rakish embodiment of what an NFL quarterback is supposed to be. His golden locks, his hell-bent style, his propensity to snatch victory from the jaws of defeat, and his ability to move beyond mistakes endeared him, at least for a little while, to Packer Backers.

His origins were ordinary enough. A solid but unspectacular quarterback at the University of Virginia, Majkowski was selected by the Packers in the tenth round of the 1987 draft and was given the opportunity to fill a job vacancy that had become a major sore spot for the Green and Gold.

Majkowski and incumbent Randy Wright waged a two-year battle for the quarterback position, but neither played well enough to lock down the job permanently. Finally, at the start of the 1989 season, coach Lindy Infante took a leap of faith and decided that Majkowski gave the

Don Majkowski, nicknamed "Majik Man" for his late-game heroics, had a fairy-tale season in 1989 but never recaptured that glory.

Packers the best chance to win. It proved to be a wise decision because what a remarkably exciting season it turned out to be!

During the 1989 season, Majkowski led the Packers to down-to-the-wire victories—all by a single point—over New Orleans, Chicago, Minnesota, and Tampa Bay. That year, Green Bay posted a 10–6 record; seven of those wins were thanks to come-from-behind rallies. Leading the circus all the way was Majkowski, who threw for 4,318 yards and 27 touchdowns, which earned him the nickname "Majik Man."

Despite posting their best record of the decade, the '89 Packers narrowly missed the playoffs. As the 1990s dawned, Majkowski began to understand just how important he was to the Packers, so he decided that he wanted a new contract and held out for a tumultuous 45 days during training camp.

But by the time Majkowski returned, just before the start of the regular season, nothing was the same. He reclaimed his starting job from Anthony Dilweg by the season's third week, but the magic, in many ways, was gone.

Majkowski struggled all season, and after a torn rotator cuff (suffered during a November 18 game against Phoenix) sent him to the sidelines, the season fell apart. The Packers dropped their final five games and finished the season 6–10.

Injuries and inconsistency plagued Majkowski in 1991, and he was benched midway through the season. In 1992, he reclaimed his starting spot under new coach Mike Holmgren, but then came the now-famous September 20 game against Cincinnati, in which Majkowski suffered torn ligaments in his right ankle. His replacement? A young and eager Brett Favre.

Majkowski left the Packers in 1993 and played two seasons each in Indianapolis and Detroit, but his ankle injury never really healed and he reluctantly retired after the 1996 season.

Majkowski was inducted into the Packers Hall of Fame in 2005. His "Majik Network" also provides radio and TV analysis of the Packers and the NFL.

A Sterling Performance

It's a story that perhaps sums up Sterling Sharpe's career with the Green Bay Packers better than any other. It was December 27, 1992, and the Packers had just lost to the Minnesota Vikings in the Metrodome, costing them a playoff berth.

But in the game, Sharpe set a team record for most receptions in a season with 108. The media was eager to talk to Sharpe about the record (which he broke the next year with 112 catches), but he was nowhere to be found.

Sharpe had been antagonistic toward the local media since it had criticized his penchant for dropping passes during his rookie season, so he stopped talking to anyone who covered the Packers. And even on this momentous occasion, Sharpe hid out in the team training room until the media finally left.

Sharpe was a perfect enigma. He played through injury for years and was adored by Packers fans. But he wouldn't sign autographs in public, and he fled to his native South Carolina the day after every season ended. Yet, every Tuesday morning during the season, he'd sign boxes of photos and respond to letters from fans—but away from prying eyes.

The seventh pick overall in the 1988 draft, Sharpe played seven rugged seasons in the NFL—all with the Packers. He caught a team-record 595 passes for 8,134 yards and 65 touchdowns, both of which rank second in team history. Sharpe flourished in the offense designed by coach Mike Holmgren and triggered by quarterback Brett Favre starting in 1992. In fact, in Sharpe's final three seasons (1992–94), he caught 108, 112, and 94 passes, respectively, and a total of 42 touchdowns.

Sterling Sharpe, Green Bay's first-round draft pick in 1988, became one of the most prolific receivers in team history. He caught 595 passes in a seven-year career that was cut short by injury.

But in 1994, Sharpe alienated many teammates when, on the day before the season opener against Minnesota, he threatened to sit out due to a contract dispute. The move enraged Favre and Holmgren, and Sharpe eventually decided to play, catching a touchdown in the 16–10 win. But he damaged more than a few relationships with the selfish move.

Perhaps Sharpe redeemed himself by playing all season with a badly injured toe that kept him from practicing. Despite the pain, he was on the field for every game and played with his usual abandon.

Then, in the season finale at Tampa Bay, Sharpe was momentarily paralyzed by a tackle. After the game, doctors discovered that he suffered from a congenital narrowing of the spinal column, and if he continued to play, he'd risk permanent paralysis. That shut him down for the playoffs, and when he tried to return in 1995, the injury was no better, so he retired.

Ironically, Sharpe, who avoided the press during his playing days, went on to a career in the media, first as a studio analyst with ESPN and then with the NFL Network. He was inducted into the Packers Hall of Fame in 2002.

Although aloof with the media, Sterling Sharpe was admired for his work ethic and his ability to play through injuries.

The Incredible Blunder

It seemed like a good idea at the time. With the second pick in the 1989 NFL draft, the Packers wanted to select a dominant offensive lineman. The first, last, and only choice was Michigan State tackle Tony Mandarich—dubbed "The Incredible Bulk"—who had been anointed by many pro scouts and NFL general managers as the best offensive lineman in draft history.

Blinded by this acclaim and Mandarich's résumé, the Packers bypassed a Heisman Trophy-winning running back from Oklahoma State named Barry Sanders, a linebacker from Alabama named Derrick Thomas, and a cornerback from Florida State named Deion Sanders to select Mandarich instead.

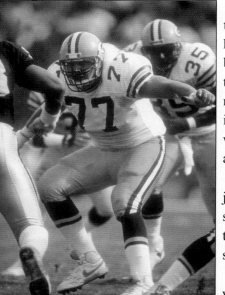

In 1989, Tony Mandarich was expected to be the NFL's next great offensive lineman. Instead, he was one of the league's biggest busts.

Almost immediately, the Packers had questions about Mandarich. Rumors of steroid use had dogged him throughout his college days, but the Packers ignored them. However, when the NFL made it clear that its policy toward the muscle-building compounds would be enforced in dramatic fashion that season, the Packers watched in horror as Mandarich grew noticeably smaller before their very eyes.

The highly touted rookie could not beat out journeyman Alan Veingrad for a starting tackle spot. He spent most of the next two seasons on the sidelines, all the while denying rumors of steroid abuse.

Finally, after the 1992 season, the Packers washed their hands of Mandarich by releasing him. Mandarich resurfaced in 1996 and played well for the Indianapolis Colts before retiring after the 1998 season.

In 2005, Mandarich finally admitted to taking steroids in college and faking drug tests, but he still says that he never took performance-enhancing drugs while in the NFL.

Light at the End of the Tunnel

If there was a day on which the Packers took their first steps back toward respectability, it was June 5, 1989. That was the day the Packers named Bob Harlan the team's president and chief executive officer.

In his 18 years with the Packers, Harlan had served in nearly every possible capacity, starting as a 34-year-old assistant

Bob Harlan has been an integral part of the Packers' organization since 1971. He now serves as chairman emeritus.

general manager in 1971 and moving on to corporate general manager in 1975, where he handled many contract negotiations. In 1981, he was named corporate assistant to team president Dominic Olejniczak, then became vice president of administration in 1988 before assuming the dual roles of president and CEO the following year.

Harlan had to make a number of tough, controversial decisions over the years, and just about every one paid dividends. He was the one who tracked down Ron Wolf, persuaded him to leave the New York Jets, and gave him complete autonomy over football operations.

He was the one who decided that, for financial reasons, the Packers had to cease playing games in Milwaukee. And he shepherded the $295 million Lambeau Field renovation that began in 2000.

Harlan maintained his role as team president and CEO until 2007, when he had hoped to retire. But when his chosen successor, John Jones, backed away, he returned to his old roles long enough to help find another replacement, Mark Murphy.

Though officially retired, Harlan remains one of the organization's most visible and popular faces and stays busy by speaking to groups around the state about his favorite topic—the Packers.

The Cardiac Pack

If the 1989 Green Bay Packers did nothing else, they provided the kind of roller-coaster, what's-going-to-happen-next entertainment that the franchise had never seen before and, frankly, hasn't seen since.

That season, nine games were decided by three points or fewer, and of those, four were one-point decisions that were decided in the last minute and a half—and all went in the Packers' favor.

The circus really got underway during the season's second week, when the Packers shook off a 24–7 halftime deficit at home against New Orleans and rallied for a 35–34 win when Don Majkowski threw a three-yard touchdown pass to Sterling Sharpe with 1:26 to play.

"That game really set the tone for the whole season," recalled Majkowski. "It was a game that was kind of forgotten, but it was an unbelievable comeback."

Majkowski was right. The Packers would make a habit of dancing on the cliff's edge every week during that season, and, more often than not, they came out on top. That was best symbolized on November 5 in a game that has come to be known as the "Instant Replay Game" or, more fondly for Packers fans, the "Upon Further Review, the Bears Still Suck Game."

The Packers trailed their hated rival 13–7 with 41 seconds to play. On fourth down from the Bears' 14-yard line, Majkowski scrambled to his right and hit Sharpe for the apparent game-winning touchdown. But line judge Jim Quirk threw a penalty flag and called Majkowski for being over the line of scrimmage.

This was during the infancy of the NFL-mandated instant replay, so the tape was

On November 5, 1989, the Packers defeated their bitter rival, the Bears, with a controversial ruling that is still contested to this day.

reviewed from high above Lambeau Field while players and fans waited. Finally, after five long minutes, it was ruled that Majkowski had not crossed the line. The stadium erupted, and the Packers won.

Coach Mike Ditka was so furious at the ruling that he ordered the Bears' public relations office to place an asterisk by the score in the team's media guide.

Sterling Sharpe (84) is mobbed by teammates after catching the winning TD pass against the New Orleans Saints on September 17, 1989.

But the season wasn't over yet. Majkowski masterminded additional late-game comebacks in back-to-back weeks over Minnesota (20–19) and Tampa Bay (17–16).

The only thing that would have made the season even more memorable was if Green Bay had secured a playoff berth. But despite a 10–6 record, the Packers missed the postseason because the Vikings (who were also 10–6) had a better conference record.

And, as it turned out, the '89 season was just a fluke. In 1990, Majkowski missed most of training camp with a bitter contract holdout and was never the same. The Pack tumbled to a 6–10 record that season and were even worse in 1991, falling to 4–12.

Two years removed from one of the most entertaining seasons in team history, coach Lindy Infante was fired and a new future awaited—again.

PACKERS PARAPHERNALIA

This sticker and button say it all. Plain and simple, Packers fans back their team no matter what the outcome.

When the Packers faced the St. Louis Cardinals in round one of the playoffs on January 8, 1983, they fell behind briefly in the first quarter. But 21 points in the second sealed the deal for the Pack in their 41–16 win.

Three Cowboys interceptions proved costly for the Packers, who went down 37–26 in round two of the playoffs on January 16, 1983.

Chester Marcol received this football to commemorate his first touchdown in the NFL. In the Packers' 1980 overtime victory against the Bears, Marcol was responsible for all 12 of the team's points—he kicked two field goals and scored the game-winning touchdown.

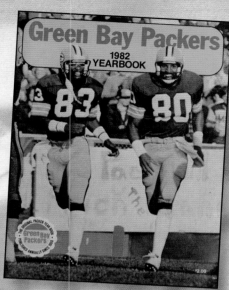

Only die-hard fans purchased Packers pennants from 1973 to '88, an era in which Green Bay never won more than eight games in a season.

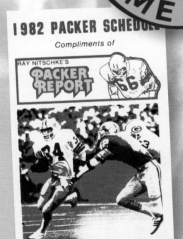

The Pack did indeed come back, with first place finishes in both 1972 and '82. But their time on top was fleeting, and they would not make it back to the playoffs until 1993.

Pro Bowlers John Jefferson (83) and James Lofton (80), along with quarterback Lynn Dickey, gave the Packers of the early '80s one of the best passing games in the business.

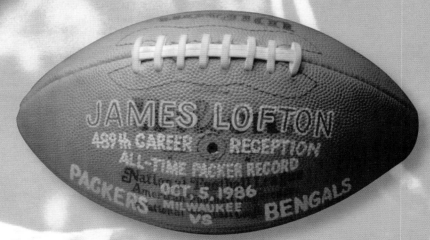

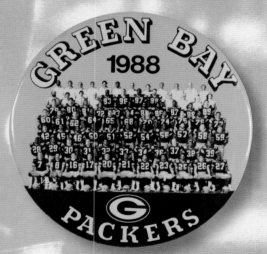

The Packers finished first in their division in 1982, but a players strike disrupted the season, so a special Super Bowl Tournament was held in lieu of the usual playoff format.

On October 5, 1986, James Lofton surpassed the legendary Don Hutson in the Packers' record book with his 489th career catch. He left the Packers at the end of the '86 season with 530 total receptions.

The '88 Packers finished a pallid 4–12 in Lindy Infante's first season at the helm. But Don Majkowski and Sterling Sharpe led the "Cardiac Pack" to better days in '89.

CHAPTER FIVE

RETURN TO TITLETOWN

1992–TODAY

"Green Bay is the football Mecca.

It's where pro football started, and the

Green Bay Packers will always be a part of it."

RON WOLF, FORMER PACKERS GENERAL MANAGER

Above: *With a victory in Super Bowl XXXI, Green Bay reclaimed the moniker Titletown, U.S.A.*
Right: *Tight end Jeff Thomason (83) lifts Brett Favre in celebration after the quarterback ran in for a score in Super Bowl XXXI. The Packers went on to defeat the New England Patriots 35–21.*

The Dynamic Duo

Bob Harlan's message to Ron Wolf in November 1991 was simple: We want to stop losing. We want to stop being the laughingstock of the NFL. And we want you to do whatever you need to do to make that happen. "I was so tired of losing," Harlan later said.

Ron Wolf, a no-nonsense football executive with nearly 30 years of experience, first caught Harlan's attention four years earlier when he interviewed for the position of Packers personnel director, a job that eventually went to Tom Braatz after Wolf pulled his name out of consideration.

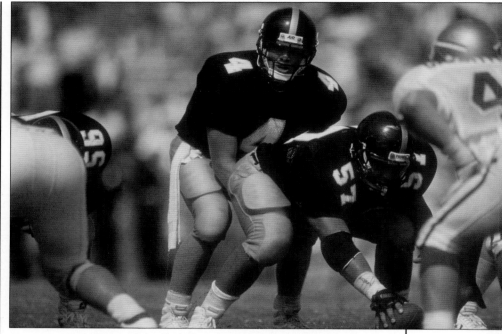

Brett Favre (4), shown here in a 1989 Southern Miss victory over Florida State, had been on Ron Wolf's radar when Wolf was director of player personnel with the New York Jets.

Now Harlan had a grander scheme. He wanted a general manager to wield the kind of authority not seen in the organization since the days of Vince Lombardi. Harlan told Wolf that whatever needed to be done, he could do it.

Unsure that he had heard this correctly, Wolf asked Harlan on more than one occasion during the interview process if he really meant what he'd said. Harlan said that he did.

It was carte blanche in terms of football issues, and it was a situation that Wolf, who was player personnel director of the New York Jets at the time, couldn't turn down. He swooped into Green Bay in late 1991 and spent the final weeks of the season evaluating everyone and everything.

Friends advised Ron Wolf not to accept the GM position in Green Bay, but he was intrigued by the opportunity and accepted Bob Harlan's offer.

As a longtime AFL and AFC executive, Wolf hadn't spent much time thinking about the Packers. And friends and associates actually warned him that going to Green Bay could be a mistake. "I didn't believe it," Wolf said.

What he found, though, was a team without discipline and a coaching staff that had lost control of its players. He also evaluated outside talent, so when the Packers traveled to Atlanta to play the Falcons on December 1, he planned to go down to the sidelines during pregame warm-ups to watch Atlanta's rookie backup quarterback, Brett Favre.

Wolf had been impressed by Favre when he saw him play at the University of Southern Mississippi, and now the wheels were turning. He wanted to see if the kid was still the standout player that he remembered.

RETURN TO TITLETOWN: 1992–TODAY

Ironically, Wolf was late getting down to the field and never saw Favre throw. But he still believed that he knew everything he needed to know.

Armed with much of the information he needed, Wolf fired Lindy Infante the day after the season ended and immediately set his sights on hiring Mike Holmgren, the hottest young coaching prospect available, who had worked wonders as offensive coordinator of the San Francisco 49ers.

Mike Holmgren took the reins as Packers head coach in 1992, and the change was felt immediately. They went from 4–12 in 1991 to 9–7 in '92.

Moving the Chains

To true believers, the term "West Coast offense" is an insult. Sure, it was born on the West Coast in the fertile minds of San Diego Chargers coach Sid Gillman and 49ers coach Bill Walsh. And, yes, it was perfected by teams on the West Coast like the 49ers. But those in the know have always bristled at the title; they're convinced that too many people think "West Coast offense" translates to "soft."

In its most basic form, the West Coast offense relies on short, precision passes to gain yardage and "move the chains" (i.e., gain first downs). It isn't the football of Vince Lombardi's time, when physical, overpowering running games dominated. The pass—especially the screen pass—is the primary weapon in the West Coast offense.

And though it may rely more on deception and short passes, proponents say that there's nothing soft about the West Coast offense—it still requires good blocking and physical play. But it also requires players, especially the quarterback, to make quick, accurate, split-second decisions. The Packers and more than half of the teams in the NFL subscribe to some form of the West Coast offense.

Holmgren was being wooed by other teams, including the Jets and the Miami Dolphins, but Holmgren saw something in Wolf, and in Green Bay, that intrigued him. Hiring Holmgren didn't come cheap, however. Annoyed that the Packers came after one of their high-profile assistants (who was still under contract), the 49ers demanded a second-round draft choice from Green Bay. Wolf gladly obliged.

By January 1992, the dynamic duo was in place, with Wolf as GM and Holmgren as the innovative head coach. Next came the task of revamping the roster, and both men knew that began—and ended, for that matter—with finding a quarterback who could run the new offense that Holmgren planned to install.

Wolf told Holmgren that he planned to give up a first-round draft choice for the kid from Atlanta. Holmgren, though not familiar with Favre, deferred to his new boss.

A plan was coming together.

The Trade

No one knew it at the time. How could they? No one knew that Ron Wolf's hunch would turn into the greatest personnel decision in Green Bay Packers history. No one could pronounce the kid's name, much less project what he would mean to the franchise and to the NFL itself.

But the feeling gnawed at Wolf for two years—ever since he'd seen Brett Favre as a junior quarterback at the University of Southern Mississippi. There was something intangible and exciting about the way Favre played the game. He played like a little kid in Pop Warner. He loved football in ways Wolf had rarely seen. And, oh, that arm!

Brett Favre poses with Atlanta Falcons head coach Jerry Glanville. Favre was the second-round draft pick of the Falcons in 1991, but he and Glanville clashed almost immediately.

"This kid had something I couldn't put my finger on. But I knew he was going to be special. Don't ask me how I knew, but I knew," Wolf recalled.

When he first saw Favre, Wolf was personnel director for the New York Jets, and he made it clear to anyone who would listen that they should draft Favre with their second-round pick in the April 1991 draft. Though others in the organization weren't as convinced—especially after Favre's unspectacular senior season, which had been hampered by a preseason car accident—they went with Wolf's recommendation and were ready to select Favre.

But one pick before the Jets were ready to take Favre with the 34th overall selection in the draft, the Falcons snatched him up. The Jets took another quarterback, Louisville's Browning Nagle, with their pick.

A year later, Wolf was running the Packers, and he knew that the quarterbacks he had on hand, led by the fading Don Majkowski, were not adequate. Wolf knew that he needed a bold, definitive stroke to make it clear that he was making changes that mattered, and acquiring Favre was high on his list. And unbelievably, considering how badly Wolf wanted Favre, the Falcons seemed just as anxious to be rid of him. The free-spirited and stubborn Favre often clashed with the team's equally free-spirited and stubborn head coach, Jerry Glanville.

Favre was miserable being relegated to a third-string quarterback, and Glanville made it clear that it would take a disaster for Favre to see playing time. "Only if the other quarterbacks on the team get in a train wreck," he cracked.

Favre's conditioning suffered and so did his attitude. He often took out his frustration in pregame warm-ups by seeing how far into the stadium's upper deck he could launch the pigskin.

So in February 1992, in a move that surprised nearly everyone, the Packers gave up their No. 1 pick in the April draft for Favre. Of course, it looks like a huge mistake on the part of Atlanta

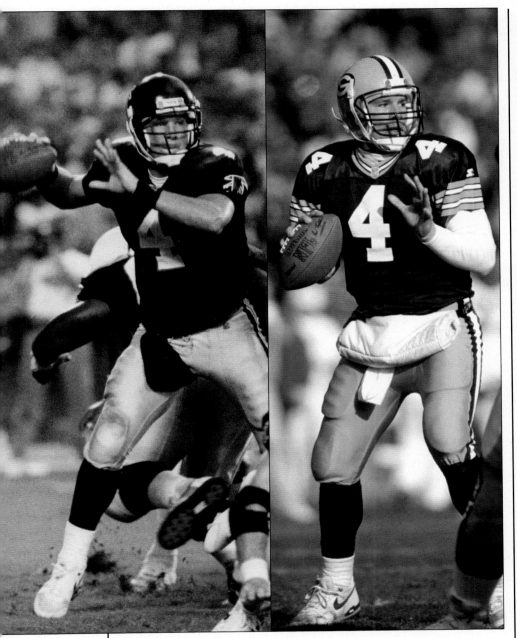

What a difference a year can make! With a coach who didn't believe in him in Atlanta, Brett Favre saw little playing time as a third-string QB. But he really shined after a trade to Green Bay, shattering numerous records and becoming perhaps the best quarterback of all time.

The Three Amigos

They could not have come from three more different places. Brett Favre, raised in the Mississippi bayou; Frank Winters, from the tough streets of New Jersey, in the shadow of New York City; and Mark Chmura, from the affluent hamlet of Deerfield, Massachusetts. But the three forged a bond that lasted for years and saddled them with the moniker "The Three Amigos."

All three joined the Packers in 1992 as part of the new Ron Wolf–Mike Holmgren regime. Favre was traded from Atlanta; Winters, a center, was a free agent acquisition from the Kansas City Chiefs; and Chmura, a tight end, was a sixth-round draft pick from Boston College.

They all suffered through Holmgren's withering criticism and need for perfection, and, as a result, they became closer than brothers. They played golf together, they hung out together—they even took vacations together, including one memorable trip to Favre's home deep in the Mississippi bayou.

The three were all but inseparable until 2000, when Chmura was charged with sexual assault. After a very public, very sordid trial, Chmura was found not guilty. But throughout the ordeal, Favre reportedly did not once contact his old friend.

now, but even Favre admitted years later that if he had been the Falcons' GM, he would have made the deal. "I would've traded me, too," he said.

But the saga wasn't quite finished. So secure was Wolf in the deal that he hadn't even drawn up a contingency plan in case Favre didn't pass a routine team physical. A few days later, that's exactly what happened—a bad shoulder and a bad knee forced team doctor Patrick McKenzie to fail Wolf's prize acquisition.

Wolf recalled years later: "I sent [Favre] back over for another physical, and I said to the doctors, 'He's going to pass.' And he did. I mean I pinned my career on this guy."

As a footnote, the Falcons spent the first-round pick they got for Favre on another Southern Mississippi player, running back Tony Smith, who lasted just three seasons in the NFL.

A White Sale

Reggie White always remembered the first time he realized that he could see himself playing for the Packers. It was a November 15, 1992, game in Milwaukee in which White and his Philadelphia Eagles mercilessly beat up on a young Brett Favre, even separating his left shoulder at one point. Still, the kid found a way to lead the Packers to a 27–24 win. "That showed me something," White said later.

A few months later, a league-wide frenzy to sign White as a free agent began. Nearly every team in the NFL wanted the services of the league's best pass-rusher, the Packers included. But Green Bay knew that they didn't possess the reputation, or the bank account, of the big hitters like the Washington Redskins and San Francisco 49ers, who also desperately wanted White and appeared to be the leaders in the race.

But White wanted to go to a team that had the potential to win a Super Bowl, and in Favre, he saw a quarterback who could make that happen. Of course, he also liked the four-year, $17 million deal that the Packers offered him; at that point, it was the third-largest contract in NFL history.

Even so, when White chose the Packers in April 1993, it stunned the league, as well as Packers fans, and, to a degree, even Ron Wolf and Mike Holmgren. Almost overnight, the widely held view of the Packers changed. Suddenly, this was a franchise to be taken seriously—it was a team with a young, talented quarterback, the league's top pass-rusher, and an innovative coaching staff that was ready to make a run at the Super Bowl.

In 1992, the Packers somehow scratched out a 9–7 record with a ragtag crew of young, untested players and a quarterback who got by on moxie, guts, and a great arm. In 1993, with Favre in his first full year as a starter and White posting a team-high 13 sacks, the Packers again finished the season 9–7 but this time earned their first playoff berth since the strike-shortened 1982 season.

In a remarkable high-wire act against the Lions in Detroit during the first round of the playoffs, Favre threw three touchdown passes to Sterling Sharpe, including the game-winner—a scrambling, across-the-body heave—with 55 seconds to play, which secured a 28–24 win. White was beaming afterward. "That's why I came here," he exclaimed.

The young Packers were brought back to earth the following week against the Dallas Cowboys—the eventual Super Bowl champions. But Green Bay held its own, and Favre threw for 331 yards and two touchdowns in the 27–17 loss.

Again, White smiled afterward, despite the loss. "We're going places," he said. "I see that."

In 1993, the Packers immediately became a force to be reckoned with when they signed defensive end Reggie White—the highest-profile free agent in the NFL at the time.

Reggie White wore No. 92 for the Packers from 1993 to 1998. The team retired No. 92 in a ceremony on September 18, 2005.

The Butler Did It

If Reggie White was the final piece of the puzzle that would take the Packers back to NFL prominence, LeRoy Butler may have been the first piece. Butler was Green Bay's second-round draft pick in 1990, during the reign of Tom Braatz and Lindy Infante, and he was a Packers defensive mainstay for 12 seasons.

Butler, a four-time All-Pro and Pro Bowler (1993, '96, '97, '98), was named to the NFL's All-Decade Team and was inducted into the Packers Hall of Fame in 2007.

Butler, who spent his entire NFL career with the Packers, recorded 953 tackles, 38 interceptions, and 20.5 sacks. Five times, he led or tied for the team lead in interceptions and was the first defensive back in league history to gain entrance into the 20 sack/20 interception club. But despite all that, Butler may be best known for inventing the now legendary "Lambeau Leap."

Its genesis came on December 26, 1993, at Green Bay's "Frozen Tundra." The Packers were routing the Los Angeles Raiders, who had already mentally checked out due to the frigid conditions. When the Raiders fumbled in the fourth quarter, Reggie White picked up the ball and lateraled it to Butler, who was trailing the play. "The crowd was going crazy," Butler recalled.

In a fit of spontaneous euphoria after scoring, Butler leaped into the bleachers behind the end zone. The crowd went wild, and a tradition was born. Within a year, the "Lambeau Leap" had become a part of Packers lore.

The beginning of the end for Butler came in 2001 when he broke a shoulder blade during a tackle. He tried to return in 2002, but the injury had not healed properly, so he called it a career.

Safety LeRoy Butler was a stalwart in the Packers' defensive backfield from 1990 to 2001 and was credited with inventing the "Lambeau Leap."

Leaping into History

Though LeRoy Butler introduced the Lambeau Leap in 1993, it didn't really take off until 1995. That season, when it was obvious that the Packers were on to something special as a franchise, nearly every player who scored a touchdown wanted to take the leap.

The best of the bunch was wide receiver Robert Brooks. The lanky South Carolina product assumed the split end spot from Sterling Sharpe, who was forced to retire with a serious injury after the 1994 season. Brooks responded with 102 receptions in 1995, and every time he scored at Lambeau, he vaulted headlong into the stands.

By 1996, the Packers had developed routines in which the guy who scored would jump in first, then two or three teammates would follow. Defensive players who scored did the leap, too. The Packers never did it during road games, though many were tempted.

The leap became so popular that players on other teams began leaping into the stands at their home stadiums, too. But it was never quite the same, and the Packers often derided the blatant copycatting.

Mike Holmgren was never thrilled with the practice because of his concern about injuries. But he ultimately accepted it as part of the Packers experience. His only warning was to Packers fans: "If they jump in," he cracked, "please throw them back."

Robert Brooks takes a leap into the Lambeau Field crowd after scoring a touchdown against the Bears in 1995.

Game Day

To those who have never been to Green Bay on a Packers game day, consider what it would be like to roll Mardi Gras, a New Year's Eve celebration, a bachelor party, and Christmas morning into one event.

It has always been that way, from the days of Hagemeister Park and the old City Stadium all the way up to the present. Every hotel room within a 40-mile radius gets booked

In a scene typical of every Packers home game, nearly 73,000 fans pack Lambeau Field to watch the Green and Gold take on the Chicago Bears in September 2004.

because season tickets to Lambeau Field have been sold out since 1960, and the waiting list for Packers season tickets now sits at more than 78,000. Each time a renovation increases the capacity of Lambeau Field, the waiting list gets smaller as more tickets are made available. But this decrease is short-lived because the number of people who want season

by April (when the Packers' schedule for the upcoming season is announced). Families plan vacations around Packers home games; weddings are moved to avoid game days.

Game day itself is a collision of sights, sounds, and smells. It is a celebratory event that happens eight times a year (not including preseason or playoff games), and fans take advantage of it.

For years, residents along Ridge Road, just north of the stadium, have opened their yards to allow fans to park. It used to cost $5. Then $10. In the Super Bowl years, the price rose to $15. Now it's $20–25.

Scalping tickets—reselling them for more than face value—is illegal in Wisconsin. But in one area across from the stadium, local officials allow fans to buy and sell tickets—sometimes for more than face value—without threat of prosecution. That's

tickets continues to grow. Season tickets are passed on to future generations in wills, are fought over in divorce settlements, and are even parts of legal settlements in bankruptcies.

Thanks to the expansive renovations of recent years, going to a Packers game is now more than just a chance to cheer for the players on the field. There are several restaurants in the stadium's atrium, an expanded Pro Shop for Packers paraphernalia, and the Packers Hall of Fame, which is a must-see for anyone visiting for the first time. Indeed, from 1996 to 1998, the Packers Hall of Fame (which was then located across the street from Lambeau Field) logged more visitors than the Pro Football Hall of Fame in Canton, Ohio.

That's because, in a sense, the history of the Packers *is* the history of the NFL. Packers history includes Curly Lambeau and

Vince Lombardi, Don Hutson and Tony Canadeo, Bart Starr and Reggie White and Brett Favre. How much more representative of the NFL does it get?

In the end, though, the organization remains what it is because of the fans. There have been four stock sales in team history—1923, 1935, 1950, and 1997, the latest of which sold more than 120,000 shares at $200 a pop. Every Packers shareholder knows that although the stock is all but worthless in terms of monetary value, that's not really the point. They own the team!

Every July, there is a meeting of stockholders at Lambeau Field, and 20,000–30,000 people usually attend because the money they spent on that stock makes each one of them part-owner of the team. During the meeting, a financial report is given, and shareholders can attend question-and-answer sessions with the team president, general manager, and head coach.

Another endearing quality of the team's ownership by the fans is that if ever there comes a point at which the Packers dissolve as an NFL franchise, all proceeds go to the Packers Foundation for distribution to local charities.

A familiar sight: Fans celebrate outside Lambeau Field prior to Green Bay's playoff game with the Seattle Seahawks in 2008.

Change of Venue

Some say that the Packers owe their survival to the city of Milwaukee. In 1933, with revenues falling, the Packers' organization made the decision to play at least one game per season in Wisconsin's largest city to help increase attendance and raise some much-needed cash.

By the mid-1950s, the Packers were playing two or three games per season in Milwaukee. But as the 1990s dawned, Lambeau Field had added luxury boxes and suites that generated much more revenue than the antiquated, 53,000-seat Milwaukee County Stadium ever could. Besides, the Packers hated traveling there and visiting teams hated it even more. So as not to obstruct views, both team benches were on the same side of the field. The locker rooms were cramped, the seats were uncomfortable, and the Packers got nothing from concession sales or parking. All told, the Packers were losing at least $1 million per game by not playing in Green Bay.

Finally, in 1994, team president Bob Harlan made the difficult decision to move out of Milwaukee, which infuriated fans from southern Wisconsin. So Harlan offered an olive branch by setting aside two home games every year for Packers season ticket holders from the Milwaukee area. It seemed to do the trick, and Milwaukee fans continue to flock to Lambeau Field for their "Gold Package" games.

The Packers marked their last game at Milwaukee County Stadium with a 21–17 victory over the Falcons in the final seconds.

No Rush to Judgment: The '94 Playoffs

Green Bay Packers defensive coordinator Fritz Shurmur's idea of a well-run defense was simple to explain but nearly impossible to perform. He always talked about defenders being like "tines of a fork"—they should have perfect spacing and position and never allow a running back to make the moves and cuts he wants to make.

In a December 31, 1994, playoff game against the Detroit Lions at Lambeau Field, Shurmur came as close to seeing that perfect defense as he ever would. For six seasons, the Packers had been tortured by the Lions' incomparable running back Barry Sanders (whom the Packers chose not to draft in 1989 in favor of Tony Mandarich). It was bad enough facing Sanders twice during the regular season as an NFC Central foe, but the Packers had also given up 169 yards to Sanders in a playoff game the year before.

Shurmur—in his first season as Green Bay's defensive coordinator after a long career with the Lions, Rams, and Cardinals— knew that the key to beating the Lions was stopping Sanders. So Shurmur spent the week calling his defense's character into question— with ends Reggie White and Sean Jones and star linebacker Bryce Paup, he knew what his defense could do, but he needed to see it consistently. That was especially important for the Detroit contest, since three days before the game, the Packers learned that star wide receiver Sterling Sharpe would not be able to play due to a serious injury.

So in a performance for the ages, Green Bay's inspired defense held Sanders to a career-low –1 yard on 13 carries and the Lions to –4 rushing yards total, an NFL playoff record that still stands.

In the mid-1990s, Fritz Shurmur helped turn Green Bay's defense into the league's best.

But that almost wasn't enough. The Packers, leading just 16–10 in the final minute, needed a final defensive stand after the Lions drove to Green Bay's 11-yard line. Although the Lions eventually pulled off a safety, the Packers still sealed a 16–12 victory, their first home playoff win since 1982.

That set up a second straight trip to Texas to face the still-dominant Cowboys. But unlike the previous season's playoff loss in the Lone Star State, after which the Cowboys admitted that they might have underestimated the Packers, Dallas was overwhelming from the start. A 94-yard touchdown pass from Troy Aikman to Alvin Harper was the backbreaker as the Cowboys rolled to a 28–9 halftime lead and an eventual 35–9 victory.

Two years, two playoff losses to the Cowboys. It was a habit of which the Packers were already growing weary.

In a wild card round playoff game on December 31, 1994, the Packers' defensive front—(from left to right) Sean Jones, Steve McMichael, Matt Brock, John Jurkovic, Don Davey, Bryce Paup, and Reggie White—held Detroit's star running back Barry Sanders to –1 yard rushing.

Making Progress

The Packers were making progress—everyone could see that. After three straight 9–7 seasons under Mike Holmgren, the Packers improved to 11–5 in 1995 and went to the playoffs for the third time in as many years.

Brett Favre prepares to uncork a pass during the NFC championship game against the Dallas Cowboys on January 14, 1996.

The reward was a second straight first-round home playoff win—a thunderous 37–20 victory over the Atlanta Falcons. But the Packers had been down this road before, having won in the opening round of the playoffs the past two seasons. The key was what they would do next, and the challenge was massive—a meeting with the defending Super Bowl champion San Francisco 49ers at Candlestick Park. It ended up being a defining moment for the Packers' franchise.

The Packers' defense dominated the high-powered 49ers offense, forcing four turnovers, including a first-quarter fumble that cornerback Craig Newsome returned 31 yards for a touchdown and a quick 7–0 lead.

The Packers played with poise, confidence, and swagger, and they controlled the game from start to finish on the way to a 27–17 win. It was easily the most important win in the Holmgren–Wolf era to that point because it proved that what they were preaching was working. It also set up, for the third straight year, a meeting with the Cowboys at Texas Stadium. But this time, it was for the NFC championship and a spot in the Super Bowl.

The Packers, now on essentially even footing talent-wise with their longtime nemeses from Dallas, led the Cowboys 27–24 after three quarters. But then Emmitt Smith rushed for two touchdowns and Brett Favre threw a disastrous interception to thwart a scoring drive in the fourth. The Cowboys had done it to the Pack again, this time knocking them off 38–27.

On the trip back from Texas, Holmgren walked the aisle of the plane telling his players to remember how much this one hurt and to use it as an impetus for the following season.

They did.

On January 14, 1996, the Packers lost to the Dallas Cowboys in the playoffs for the third straight year.

What a Rush

Eight players in Packers history have rushed for more than 1,000 yards in a season:

1949: Tony Canadeo—208 carries, 1,052 yards
1960: Jim Taylor—230 carries, 1,101 yards
1961: Jim Taylor—243 carries, 1,307 yards
1962: Jim Taylor—272 carries, 1,474 yards
1963: Jim Taylor—248 carries, 1,018 yards
1964: Jim Taylor—235 carries, 1,169 yards
1971: John Brockington—216 carries, 1,105 yards
1972: John Brockington—274 carries, 1,027 yards
1973: John Brockington—265 carries, 1,144 yards
1978: Terdell Middleton—284 carries, 1,116 yards
1995: Edgar Bennett—316 carries, 1,067 yards
1997: Dorsey Levens—329 carries, 1,435 yards
1999: Dorsey Levens—279 carries, 1,034 yards
2000: Ahman Green—263 carries, 1,175 yards
2001: Ahman Green—304 carries, 1,387 yards
2002: Ahman Green—286 carries, 1,240 yards
2003: Ahman Green—355 carries, 1,883 yards
2004: Ahman Green—259 carries, 1,163 yards
2006: Ahman Green—266 carries, 1,059 yards
2008: Ryan Grant—312 carries, 1,203 yards
2009: Ryan Grant—282 carries, 1,253 yards

Mission Accomplished!

The Green Bay Packers gathered to start the 1996 season with only one acceptable goal in mind—winning the Super Bowl. Though coach Mike Holmgren forbade his players from talking about it specifically, it's what every player privately expected. This team, they all felt, was too good, too experienced, and too driven not to get to pro football's biggest game.

The only question—and it was a huge one—was if Brett Favre would be the same player he was in 1995. During the off-season, Favre jolted the Packers and the NFL by announcing that he was hooked on the prescription painkiller Vicodin. He spent 45 days in a rehabilitation facility in Topeka, Kansas, shaking not only that demon but also his dangerous love of alcohol.

Favre emerged refreshed and renewed just before training camp, and Holmgren, in a carefully choreographed press conference, sat to the left of his quarterback as Favre talked about the rehab and his recovery. When the press conference was over, Holmgren made it clear to everyone in the packed media hall that the subject was dead and buried.

Still, questions swirled as to whether Favre could be the player he was the year before, when he was named the league's MVP after throwing for 4,413 yards and 38 touchdowns. "Bet against me," is all Favre would say.

Some were willing to. Most were not.

Indeed, in a season-opening 34–3 thumping of the Tampa Bay Buccaneers, Favre completed 20 of 27 passes for 247 yards and four touchdowns. For the quarterback, it was sweet vindication. For the Packers as a team, it was further evidence that they were indeed the squad to beat in the NFC.

Reggie White chose the Packers as a free agent in 1993 because he felt they would soon be Super Bowl contenders. Here, he celebrates that championship.

Green Bay roared through the 1996 regular season, posting a 13–3 record. Favre won a second straight NFL MVP Award by throwing for 3,899 yards and 39 touchdowns, and the defense, behind Reggie White's 8.5 sacks, allowed just 210 points, the fewest in the league.

After a first-round bye, the Packers dominated the 49ers 35–14 in a cold, driving rainstorm at Lambeau Field. The hero of the game was Desmond Howard, a former Heisman Trophy winner who had fallen short of expectations with both the Washington Redskins and Jacksonville Jaguars before practically begging the Packers for a chance to prove himself.

In 1996, Howard was the NFL's most dangerous punt returner, bringing back three punts for touchdowns and averaging a remarkable 15 yards per return. Against the 49ers in the playoffs, he returned one punt 71 yards for a score and another 46 yards to set up another touchdown. The victory brought the NFC championship game to Green Bay for the first time since the 1967 "Ice Bowl." And the weather was all too familiar—clear and bitterly cold with a windchill of –17 degrees.

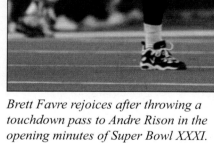

Brett Favre rejoices after throwing a touchdown pass to Andre Rison in the opening minutes of Super Bowl XXXI.

After a slow start, the Packers pounded away on the young Carolina Panthers, eventually piling up 479 total yards and winning 30–13. Afterward, before a raucous Lambeau crowd that refused to leave, Favre and White embraced.

"Thanks," White said.

"You're welcome," Favre replied.

But the job wasn't finished. For the first time in 29 years, the Packers were back in the Super Bowl. They would face the New England Patriots and their wily veteran coach Bill Parcells at the Superdome in New Orleans.

Though the Packers praised the Patriots publicly, a number of players privately thought that the match-up favored Green Bay. And, in the end, they were right. Favre threw for 246 yards and two touchdowns, Howard returned a kickoff 99 yards for another score (and was named the Super Bowl MVP), and White posted three sacks as Green Bay won its first NFL championship in nearly three decades by a score of 35–21.

In an emotional postgame speech to his players, Holmgren's voice caught as he said, "As much as this trophy means to every other team in the league, it means more to us."

The Vince Lombardi Trophy was back where it belonged—in Green Bay.

Head coach Mike Holmgren is carried off the field in triumph after the Packers defeated the New England Patriots in Super Bowl XXXI.

A Hero's Welcome

Packers fans had waited decades for a championship, and a little snowstorm wasn't going to interfere with their celebration. The victorious Packers returned home the day after winning the franchise's third Super Bowl, and the celebration plan that was in place seemed simple enough: The players would travel by bus the five miles or so from Green Bay's airport to Lambeau Field for a ceremony with the fans.

Despite the snow and –20 degree temperature, the route was clogged with thousands of fans, who slowed the buses down to a crawl. In many cases, fans climbed up the sides of the buses to shake hands with the players, who smiled and waved. Finally, three hours later, the team arrived at Lambeau Field, which had been packed several hours before the team plane even landed.

"You people are crazy," wide receiver Don Beebe joked as he triumphantly held up the Lombardi Trophy.

"This is for you," Holmgren thundered, also displaying the trophy to the crowd. The noise was deafening, but it was music to the ears of the Packers and their fans.

Thousands of people choked the Packers' parade route from the Green Bay airport to Lambeau Field, turning a 15-minute trip into a two-hour trek.

Like this pennant says, the 1996 Green Bay Packers were Super Bowl champions.

Defensive end Sean Jones holds the Lombardi Trophy in one hand and his son Dylan in the other on the front page of the January 27, 1997, Press-Gazette.

Above: The Green Bay Press-Gazette issued this poster to salute the Packers' 1996 NFC championship. The victory made them Super Bowl-bound.

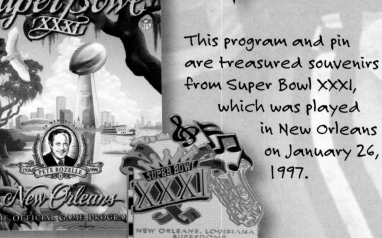

This program and pin are treasured souvenirs from Super Bowl XXXI, which was played in New Orleans on January 26, 1997.

Packers fans proudly waved their "title towels" in honor of their Super Bowl champion team.

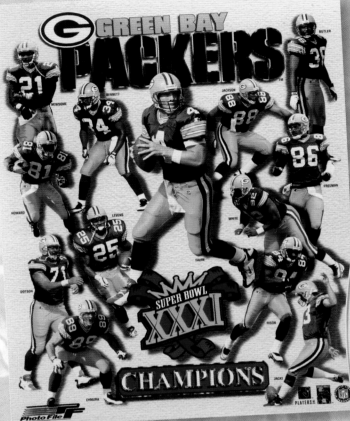

This poster and mug commemorate the '96 Packers, who beat the Patriots in Super Bowl XXXI to become world champs once again.

The front page of the Milwaukee Journal Sentinel says it all: After 29 years the Lombardi Trophy was back home.

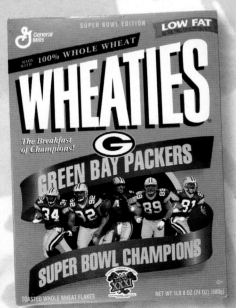

In early 1997, Wheaties—"The Breakfast of Champions"—celebrated the Super Bowl champion Green Bay Packers with a special-edition box.

This pennant hails the Packers as three-time Super Bowl champs and notes their 12 NFL titles—the most in league history.

An Opportunity Missed

Ron Wolf had built the Green Bay Packers to endure. He wanted a dynasty, and he longed for the legacy of having built a team to rival the 49ers of the 1980s, the Steelers of the 1970s, and, yes, the Packers of the 1960s. But to do that, the Packers needed to win multiple Super Bowl championships.

On paper, the 1997 Packers were stronger than the world champions of 1996. They had more experience on both sides of the ball—Seth Joyner, a Pro Bowl linebacker, came over from the Eagles to strengthen an already terrific defense, and Brett Favre was at the height of his game. In short, many predicted that the Packers would be defending their title in Super Bowl XXXII in San Diego and would beat whomever the AFC threw at them.

And they did nothing prior to the Super Bowl to suggest otherwise. They rolled through another 13–3 season, beat the tough Buccaneers 21–7 in the opening round of the playoffs, and, for the third straight season, knocked off the 49ers, this time in a driving rainstorm in San Francisco.

So, not surprisingly, the Packers returned to the Super Bowl—right where everyone expected them to be—to face the Denver Broncos, who were 13-point underdogs to the powerful Pack. But those predictions bothered head coach Mike Holmgren, who already sensed complacency and overconfidence among his players.

Tyrone Davis sits on the bench in disbelief after the Packers lost to the Broncos 31–24 in Super Bowl XXXII.

Taking Stock...Again

Success comes at a price. The Packers had one of the best teams in football, and the players wanted to be paid accordingly. But because of the organization's unusual financial makeup, which did not include a deep-pocketed owner, the money didn't just fall from the sky.

Sensing that the popularity of the Packers was at an all-time high, team president Bob Harlan announced that the fourth stock sale in team history would be held in November 1997. This time, fans could purchase stock in the team for $200 a share. Again, as in the past, the stock was essentially worthless (there were no dividends, for example) except that the certificate of ownership came with a chance to attend the annual stockholder's meeting and the knowledge that the holder owned a part of the team.

This 1997 stock certificate signifies that the shareholder is part-owner of the Green Bay Packers.

Worthless piece of paper or not, the stock sold like hotcakes. Packer Backers once again answered the call, buying 120,010 shares, which supplemented the team coffers with more than $24 million.

The Broncos, who played loose and without care, used running back Terrell Davis (157 yards, three TDs) to run the ball down the Packers' throats and build a 31–24 lead in the fourth quarter. The Packers mounted a final rally and got as far as the Broncos' 31-yard line. But Favre's fourth-down pass to tight end Mark Chmura fell incomplete, and the Broncos' upset was complete.

Afterward, Wolf was disconsolate. His vision of a Packers dynasty was, for all practical purposes, over, and when asked about the Packers' NFC dominance during the past two seasons, he said simply, "We're a one-year wonder, just a fart in the wind."

Changes Are Coming

You could feel it as surely as you can feel the change in the weather. By 1998, something was different about the Green Bay Packers. They were still a good—maybe even great—team, but many of the players felt that they had let a terrific opportunity slip away the previous January in San Diego. They all knew that the window of opportunity stayed open for only so long before it was time for the next dominant team to take over.

But perhaps the most troubling development was the status of coach Mike Holmgren, who had spent much of Super Bowl week deflecting rumors that he was in the running to become the head coach and general manager of the Seattle Seahawks.

It was long known that Holmgren wanted the titles and prestige that came with being both head coach *and* general manager, and he knew that as long as Ron Wolf controlled the reins, that wouldn't happen in Green Bay.

Holmgren had been in Green Bay for seven years. He'd won one Super Bowl and should have won a second, and he knew that there was little more for him to accomplish with the Packers. To make matters worse, Holmgren never came out and said that he wasn't interested in moving on to a position with more power.

Against that backdrop, 1998 wasn't the most comfortable season in team history. The Packers played well, for the most part, but also had shocking lapses, such as a 37–24 loss to the rising powerhouse Minnesota Vikings on October 5, which snapped Green Bay's team-record 25-game home winning streak.

Later in the season, as the team left the field at halftime during a poor performance against the woeful Philadelphia Eagles at Lambeau Field, Holmgren got into a shouting match with a fan, who accused the coach of not putting all his efforts into the game.

Nevertheless, the Packers managed an 11–5 regular season. They returned to the playoffs for the sixth straight season, and, for the fourth straight year, they faced the 49ers in the postseason.

But rumors continued to dog Holmgren in the playoffs, when it was reported that he would assume control of the 49ers—his hometown team—if then-coach Steve Mariucci didn't beat the Packers that weekend.

In a terrific game, Brett Favre directed a late drive that gave Green Bay a 27–23 lead with 1:56 to play. But the 49ers came right back, and with only three seconds to play, quarterback Steve Young threw a 25-yard touchdown pass to Terrell Owens to give San Francisco the 30–27 win.

Less than a week later, Holmgren accepted the GM/head coach job with the Seahawks, and Reggie White announced his retirement. Another era of Packers history had come to a close.

With just three seconds to play in an NFC wild card playoff game on January 3, 1999, 49ers wide receiver Terrell Owens catches the winning touchdown amidst three Packers defenders. It would be Mike Holmgren's last game as head coach of the Packers.

Rugged Rhodes

After the departure of Mike Holmgren, Ron Wolf believed that he needed to make a quick, decisive move to name a replacement. His gaze fell exclusively on Philadelphia Eagles head coach Ray Rhodes, whose intense, blunt style, Wolf thought, was just right for these Packers, whom he was convinced still had championship ability.

Ray Rhodes took over as the Packers' head coach in 1999, but it was a bad fit from the start.

Just three days after Holmgren resigned in January 1999, Wolf announced Rhodes's hiring, calling him the "perfect" fit for Green Bay. Rhodes had no designs on any more power than what he was being offered—he was a coach, not a general manager. And without Holmgren's considerable shadow looming, Wolf could conduct business the way he saw fit.

But there were red flags regarding Rhodes. He'd spent two seasons in Green Bay (1992–93) as Holmgren's defensive coordinator but took a position with the 49ers after making it clear that his family wasn't happy in Green Bay.

What's more, the year before being hired by Wolf, Rhodes led the Eagles through a disastrous season in which players, sources said, simply stopped listening to him. But Wolf ignored it all.

Yet when Wolf returned from a recruiting trip to watch a late-season practice, he was stunned. He saw players sitting on their helmets, walking to drills, and not listening to coaches. "The team was dead," Wolf said later. "For whatever reason, the players just didn't respond to Ray."

Green Bay limped to an 8–8 record, its worst since 1991, and missed the playoffs for the first time since 1992. On January 2, 2000, shortly after the last game of the season, Wolf fired Rhodes, despite giving him just one year on the job.

"It just didn't work out," said Wolf, who vowed to take more time to decide on the next hire.

Despite posting an 8–8 record and nearly leading the Packers to the playoffs, Ray Rhodes was fired after just one season.

An Unhappy Quarterback

Brett Favre and Mike Holmgren had always had a love-hate relationship. But Favre knew how important Holmgren had been to his development into the game's best quarterback.

So when Ray Rhodes—a defensive specialist—took over, Favre felt more than a little lost. He continued to perform superbly, but he grew concerned about the team's direction after a miserable 31–10 road loss to the Denver Broncos on October 17, 1999, which dropped the Packers to 3–2.

On the plane ride home from Denver, Favre sat with Ron Wolf and expressed his concerns about Rhodes and the play-calling. Two weeks later, after the Packers were embarrassed by Holmgren's Seattle Seahawks 27-7 at Lambeau Field, Favre's worries mounted.

Late in the season, defensive captain LeRoy Butler also went to Wolf with concerns about Rhodes and his handling of the defense. Butler was so upset that he did something he'd never done before—he stopped talking to the media for fear he'd say something that he'd later regret.

The New Guy

Ron Wolf admitted to anyone and everyone that his decision to hire Ray Rhodes was a mistake. He had moved too quickly, made too many assumptions, and, perhaps, thought that because most of his decisions as general manager had worked out, this one would, too.

It didn't, and, this time, Wolf vowed to take his time and find the right person.

It appeared that person would be coaching veteran Marty Schottenheimer, who had coached the Cleveland Browns and Kansas City

In a shocking decision, Ron Wolf (left) hired the relatively unknown Mike Sherman as the Packers' new head coach in 2000.

Chiefs and was looking for employment. But Schottenheimer's asking price (which was rumored to be $4 million per season) was prohibitive, and Wolf wasn't convinced that Schottenheimer was even a good fit. And with the specter of Rhodes still hanging over the franchise, Wolf had to be sure.

One of the potential coaches Wolf interviewed was Mike Sherman, who had served as the Packers' tight ends coach in 1997 and '98 before moving on to Seattle with Mike Holmgren, where he became offensive coordinator.

Wolf was blown away by Sherman's preparation and knowledge of the game and was especially impressed that he had notebooks full of practice schedules and regimens. The next morning, Wolf spoke to Bob Harlan at Lambeau Field. "If I had any guts," Wolf said, "I'd hire Sherman right now."

Harlan said, "Why not?" Five minutes later, Wolf was back in Harlan's office. "It's done," he said.

The announcement came on January 18, 2000, and, once again, it took Packers fans and much of the NFL by surprise. But unlike Rhodes, Sherman immediately understood his role as the Packers' head coach. For example, during renovations of Lambeau Field, when Sherman learned that part of the door frame from Vince Lombardi's office was still embedded in a wall in the old administration building, he asked maintenance workers to dig it out and add it to the door frame of his new office. "I want some of Coach Lombardi to rub off on me," he said.

Sherman's first season was a nondescript 9–7 affair that once again saw Green Bay miss the playoffs. But in January 2001, Wolf shocked everyone by announcing his retirement and recommending that Sherman become general manager as well as head coach. Harlan and the executive committee agreed.

Ironically, this power was what Holmgren had sought, and had he waited two years, he would have had it. Instead, Sherman, the quiet New Englander, now wielded more power than any Packers head coach since Vince Lombardi.

Mike Sherman had been Green Bay's tight ends coach for two years, but had spent the 1999 season as offensive coordinator of the Seattle Seahawks under Mike Holmgren.

Close Calls

It may have been Ron Wolf's final victory over Mike Holmgren. By 2000, Holmgren was entrenched as general manager and coach of the Seattle Seahawks, and he'd had enough of running back Ahman Green, a talented runner who had a penchant for fumbling. And nothing drove Holmgren crazier than fumbles.

So in mid-April, Holmgren dealt Green and a fifth-round draft pick that season to the Packers for under-achieving, oft-injured cornerback Fred Vinson and a sixth-round pick. It was a steal for the Packers. Vinson was injured again during training camp and was out of football a year later, while Green became one of the best running backs in Packers history. In his first season with the Packers, Green rushed for 1,175 yards, which was then the fourth-highest total in team history. And he was just getting warmed up.

In 2001, Green ran for 1,387 yards, then the second-highest single-season total in team history behind Dorsey Levens's 1,435 yards in 1997. With Green's help, the Pack rolled to a 12–4 record and returned to the playoffs after a two-year absence.

The Packers' first-round playoff opponent was their frequent postseason foe, the San Francisco 49ers. But with home-field advantage, Green Bay prevailed 25–15. However, the team's season came to a jarring conclusion the following week when the St. Louis Rams forced eight turnovers—including six Favre interceptions—and embarrassed the Packers 45–17.

In 2003, Ahman Green set a Packers record with a single-season mark of 1,883 rushing yards.

An Expensive Face-lift

LAMBEAU FIELD
VOTE
YES
SEPTEMBER 12

Brown County residents displayed signs like this one to back a tax increase that would finance a Lambeau Field renovation.

Success on the field did not necessarily translate to the bottom line for the Packers. Despite routine sellouts, Lambeau Field was not able to keep pace financially with new stadiums around the league that offered luxury boxes and suites.

By 1999, team president Bob Harlan knew that either the Packers needed a new, bigger stadium with all the bells and whistles, or venerable Lambeau Field needed a major overhaul. Harlan decided to renovate the old stadium at a cost of $295 million. (A new stadium, he was told, would cost at least $600 million.)

The project would add more seats and luxury boxes, as well as a new atrium that would house restaurants, banquet rooms, the Packers Pro Shop, and the Packers Hall of Fame, all of which would be open year-round.

But it wasn't an easy sell, since it would cost Brown County residents a 0.5 percent sales tax hike. The referendum was voted upon in September 2000, and though early numbers suggested that it would fail, 53 percent of the voters backed the plan. Lambeau Field was about to get a face-lift.

The Packers were right back in the mix the following season. Green ran for 1,240 yards, Favre threw for nearly 3,700 yards, and the Packers again posted a 12–4 regular-season record.

But against the young Atlanta Falcons at Lambeau Field in the first round of the playoffs, the Packers came out flat, trailed 24–0 at halftime, and were beaten 27–7. It was the first time that the Packers had ever lost a playoff game at Lambeau Field.

Two great regular seasons had ended with devastating playoff losses. Was this becoming a trend?

For Dad

No one meant more to Brett Favre than his dad, Irv. "Big Irv" introduced Brett to football, taught him all about the game as a kid, and was his high school coach. Irv was Brett's sounding board, his confidant, his toughest critic, and his best friend. Irv rarely missed a Packers game, and when he did, Brett always called him that night to let the old man know how it went.

On Sunday, December 22, 2003, Favre and the Packers were in Oakland preparing for a key Monday night game against the Raiders when Favre's wife Deanna called her husband's best friend, backup quarterback Doug Pederson. She told Pederson that Irv had suffered a fatal heart attack while driving near the family home in southern Mississippi.

Pederson relayed the news to Brett, and it quickly disseminated throughout the team hotel. His dad, his driving force, was gone, and Brett was 2,300 miles away preparing to play a game that the Packers *had* to win if they had any hope of making the playoffs.

Coach Mike Sherman told Favre to do what he needed to do, and if that meant leaving the team to be with his grieving mother and family, so be it. But Favre chose to stay, play, and return home the next day.

Just hours after learning that his father had passed away, Brett Favre threw for 399 yards and four touchdowns in a 41–7 thrashing of the Raiders.

What Favre did that Monday night was a study in determination and courage that is rarely seen. Playing the game of his life, Favre threw for 399 yards and four touchdowns as the Packers routed the Raiders 41–7. The performance added another layer to the growing Favre legacy, and it also helped secure home-field advantage in the first round of the playoffs against Mike Holmgren's Seahawks.

The Packers struggled with the Seahawks, who scored late and forced overtime. But barely four minutes into OT, Seahawks quarterback Matt Hasselbeck threw an ill-advised pass that was intercepted by Al Harris and returned 52 yards for the winning touchdown. That sent the Packers to Philadelphia to face the NFC's top-seeded Eagles, with the winner earning a spot in the NFC title game.

The Packers led the Eagles 17–14 with just over two minutes left in the game. The Eagles seemed lifeless, facing a fourth down and 26 from their own 25-yard line. But incredibly, quarterback Donovan McNabb completed a 28-yard pass to Freddie Mitchell to pick up the first down. A few plays later, David Akers kicked a 37-yard field goal to send the game into overtime.

During OT, Favre was intercepted by Brian Dawkins, and Akers kicked a 31-yard field goal to give the Eagles a 20–17 win. The loss was devastating for the Packers and their fans, who even today talk about "fourth and 26" and shake their heads in disgust.

Brett Favre sits forlorn on the bench after the Packers fell to the Eagles 20–17 in overtime in the playoffs on January 11, 2004.

Turbulent Times

On the football field, Brett Favre was always in control—it was off the field where things got interesting for him. In March 2000, for example, he spent a harrowing half hour crouched in an underground shelter with his young daughter Breleigh as a tornado roared across his property, destroying nearly everything in sight.

But times were especially tough for Favre starting in late 2003 and extending into 2004. It began in December 2003 when his beloved father, Irv, died of a heart attack at age 58. In 2004, more troubles found Favre and his family. On October 6, his brother-in-law Casey Tynes was killed in an ATV accident on Brett's property in Hattiesburg, Mississippi. Then, just a few days later, Favre's wife Deanna was diagnosed with breast cancer. In a show of solidarity with his ailing wife, Favre shaved his head, and he's kept his hair short ever since.

Instead of wallowing in the tragedies, Favre just kept playing football. The Packers won their third straight division title with a 10–6 record in 2004, and Favre threw for 30 touchdowns and 4,088 yards, then the fourth-highest total in his Packers career.

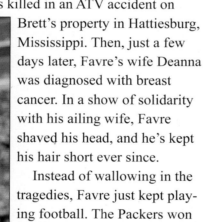

The death of lovable Reggie White was a shock to the entire NFL community. Here, he acknowledges the Lambeau Field faithful after the Packers defeated the Bears on November 12, 1995.

Giving Back

From 2000 to 2007, Brett Favre held an annual celebrity softball game to benefit his Brett Favre Fourward Foundation.

Brett and Deanna Favre have long been known for their charitable work both in Green Bay and in their native Mississippi. Favre is especially proud of his Brett Favre Fourward Foundation, which dispenses money for charities in both locations. Established in 1996, the Fourward Foundation has raised nearly $4 million thanks to a celebrity golf tournament that's held each summer in Mississippi and an annual softball game in Wisconsin.

Since 2000, sellout crowds have come to watch the charity softball game, which features Packers players and coaches. Even when a violent thunderstorm threatened to cancel the game in 2001, the faithful fans stayed, and the game was played.

The Deanna Favre Hope Foundation was established in 2004 to benefit breast cancer research. To date, it has raised more than $1 million.

But another strong season ended in crushing disappointment when the Packers hosted the Minnesota Vikings in the playoffs. They had already beaten the Vikes twice that season, but despite a raucous Lambeau Field crowd, the Packers played uninspired football. Favre threw four interceptions, and the Vikings posted a 31–17 upset victory. Couple that tough defeat with the news that former Packer Reggie White had died of a congenital lung ailment three days earlier at age 43, and it was the capper to a season that, in many ways, was better left forgotten.

Viking Conquests

The Green Bay Packers' most intense, most bitter, most hated rival these days may just be the Minnesota Vikings. Granted, such talk is heresy among longtime Packers fans, who still consider the Chicago Bears to be the team's first, last, and only antagonist.

Through 2008, the overall series record favors Green Bay 49–45–1, but if recent seasons are any indication, a rivalry doesn't get much hotter than Packers–Vikings. It's been a series that's featured taunts, accusations, cheap shots, and terrific performances—in short, everything that makes for a great rivalry.

The current rivalry was perhaps ignited on a rainy Monday night at Lambeau Field in October 1998. That night, the cocky young Vikings shattered the Packers' mystique. Despite the fact that they had been the NFC's best team each of the past two years and started the 1998 season 4–0, Green Bay had no answer for the Vikings' offense, which rang up 545 total yards. The 37–24 defeat brought the Packers' 25-game home winning streak to a screeching halt.

The series heated up even more in 2000, when the two teams went into overtime on another rainy Monday night in Green Bay. Facing third down, quarterback Brett Favre heaved a pass toward wide receiver Antonio Freeman, who fell trying to make the catch. The ball rolled along Freeman's body, and he grabbed it before it could touch the ground. Since no Viking had touched him while he was down, Freeman got up and ran 43 yards for an amazing touchdown and the 26–20 win.

Vikings defender Cris Dishman dismissed the Packers' victory as "lucky."

In 2002, Favre and Vikings defensive end Chris Hovan got into a heated argument when Hovan threatened to injure Favre.

Two years later, Green Bay frustrated the Vikings twice during the regular season by winning a pair of 34–31 decisions on last-second Ryan Longwell field goals. Then, at Lambeau during the playoffs that same season, Minnesota beat Green Bay 31–17, and

Vikings wide receiver Randy Moss showed his distaste for Packers fans by pretending to drop his pants and moon the crowd.

The heated rivalry even spilled over to the teams' front offices. In 2006, when both the Packers and Vikings were looking for new head coaches, Brad Childress interviewed in Minnesota and was set to visit Green Bay the next day. But Vikings officials signed Childress before he even had the chance to talk to Packers execs. That same year, two longtime Packers—Longwell and safety Darren Sharper— left Green Bay as free agents and signed with the Vikings.

In 2008, the Packers accused the Vikings of pursuing Favre. The NFL dismissed the charge, but the bad blood was still there. So, when Favre was traded to the New York Jets shortly thereafter, the Packers included a "poison pill" that stipulated that if the Jets traded Favre to the Vikings, New York would owe Green Bay three first-round draft picks.

On January 9, 2005, Vikings wide receiver Randy Moss taunted the Lambeau Field crowd by pretending to moon them after scoring a touchdown in the Vikings' 31–17 playoff win.

Stars of the Era

Antonio Freeman was known for his acrobatic grabs on the gridiron.

Antonio Freeman was the Packers' third-round draft pick in 1995. He left after the 2001 season, spent 2002 in Philadelphia, returned to Green Bay in 2003, and retired after the season.

From 1996 to 1999, Freeman caught 295 passes for 4,674 yards and 41 touchdowns. In 1998 alone, he caught 84 passes for an NFL-high 1,424 yards and 14 touchdowns. He was also named to the Pro Bowl and earned All-Pro honors that season.

Freeman finished his Packers career with 431 receptions (fifth in team history) for 6,651 yards (sixth in team history) and 57 touchdowns (third in team history). He was inducted into the Packers Hall of Fame in 2009.

Dorsey Levens signed a one-day contract to retire as a Packer in 2006.

Another draft-day steal perpetrated by general manager Ron Wolf, **Dorsey Levens** was a fifth-round pick out of Georgia Tech in 1994.

Levens got his first real opportunity with the team in 1995, when he played fullback. In 1996, he split time at halfback with Edgar Bennett and rushed for 566 yards. In 1997, after Bennett sustained a season-ending injury in training camp, Levens ran for 1,435 yards and scored seven rushing touchdowns; he also caught 53 passes for another 370 yards and five touchdowns and was named to the Pro Bowl.

But after that terrific season, Levens was plagued by injuries, and the Packers released him after the 2001 season. He bounced around to various teams, but he was never the same player that he was in Green Bay. He signed a one-day contract with the Packers in 2006 and retired with his original team. Levens finished his Packers career with 3,937 rushing yards and 271 receptions. He was inducted into the Packers Hall of Fame in 2009.

Desmond Howard spent only one season in Green Bay—but what a season it was! The 1991 Heisman Trophy-winning wide receiver from Michigan had mediocre stints with the Washington Redskins (1992–94) and Jacksonville Jaguars (1995) before he practically begged the Packers for an opportunity in 1996. But Howard didn't initially impress the Packers either, especially when he was sidelined for most of the preseason with a hip injury. Still, he secured a roster spot and eventually became the NFL's most dangerous kick returner that season, leading the league in punt returns (58), punt return yardage (875), and average yards per return (15.1 yards). In the playoffs, he returned one punt 71 yards for a touchdown and another 46 yards to set up another TD.

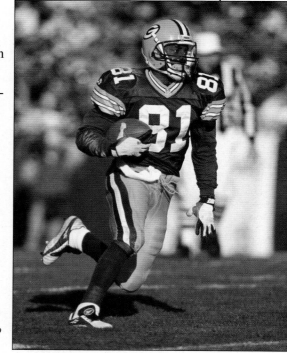

Desmond Howard won the Super Bowl XXXI MVP Award thanks to a 99-yard kickoff return.

In Super Bowl XXXI, he returned a kickoff 99 yards for a score to give Green Bay an insurmountable lead. His combined return yardage of 244 yards tied a Super Bowl record and earned him MVP honors—the first, and thus far only, time a special teams player has won the award.

Howard felt that he could parlay his success in '96 into a bigger deal, so he signed with the Oakland Raiders in 1997; that year, he led the NFL in kick returns (61). He returned to the Packers in 1999 but was traded to the Detroit Lions at midseason. He retired after the 2002 season.

Gilbert Brown was one of the most popular, yet underrated, players in recent team history. Nicknamed "The Gravedigger," Brown played nose tackle and was one of the preeminent run stoppers in the league.

A third-round draft choice by the Minnesota Vikings in 1993, Brown was released by the Vikes because his weight, which reportedly ballooned to 355 pounds, was a major concern. The Packers picked him up, and after two unremarkable seasons, he took his place on a defensive line that also featured tackle Santana Dotson and ends Reggie White and Sean Jones.

Brown also endeared himself to the fans when, after his exceptional 1996 season, he turned down a larger offer from Jacksonville to stay in Green Bay. He played for the Packers through 1999,

Gilbert Brown earned his nickname, "The Grave-digger," as a result of the dance he performed to celebrate a momentous tackle.

but a contract dispute caused him to sit out the 2000 season. He returned in 2001 and played for the Packers through 2003; he was released at the end of that season.

In Brown's 125 games with the Packers, he racked up 292 tackles and seven sacks. He was inducted into the Packers Hall of Fame in 2008.

Ryan Longwell didn't really stand a chance when he arrived at Packers training camp in 1997. He was a "camp leg"—a guy brought in to take some of the pressure off the man who was supposed to be Green Bay's new field goal kicker, third-round draft pick Brett Conway.

But Conway was injured during training camp and Longwell, an undrafted free agent from the University of California, took over and never let go. For the next nine seasons, he was the Packers' most reliable kicker, collecting 226 field goals and 1,054 points, both of which are team records.

Much to the chagrin of Packer Backers, Longwell left Green Bay after the 2005 season and signed as a free agent with the Minnesota Vikings.

Kicker Ryan Longwell came to the Packers as a free agent in 1997 and eventually became the team's all-time leading scorer with 1,054 points.

Time for Thompson

Mike Sherman never set out to be both the head coach and general manager of the Packers. But when Ron Wolf retired after the 2000 season and recommended Sherman for the job, he did not shrink from the task.

It's the kind of power every coach in the NFL—and, really, every pro sport—would love to have. Select the personnel and coach it—what more can you ask for?

But it's not easy, as Mike Holmgren learned in Seattle when he was stripped of his GM title after the 2002 season. Sherman also discovered this when, after some puzzling draft decisions, team president Bob Harlan took the general manager title away from him after the 2004 season.

It was a decision that Sherman accepted—he didn't have much of a choice—but he didn't necessarily agree with it. His replacement was Ted Thompson, who played for the Houston Oilers in the late 1970s and then moved into Green Bay's front office,

where he became a Wolf protégé and was involved in player personnel decisions for eight seasons. He moved on to Seattle with Holmgren in 1999 to become the Seahawks' vice president of football operations.

But when the opportunity to move back to Green Bay as general manager presented itself, Thompson jumped at it. Low-key and unflappable, he was viewed by most NFL observers as a terrific evaluator of personnel. He wasted little time putting his stamp on the franchise, as he let go of three key veterans—guards Mike Wahle and Marco Rivera and safety Darren Sharper—because he chose not to meet their contract demands. The next off-season, Thompson let kicker and all-time leading scorer Ryan Longwell sign with Minnesota for the same reason.

After the 2005 season, Brett Favre began to question his dedication to the game.

On January 15, 2005, Ted Thompson assumed the role of executive vice president and director of football operations. He replaced Mike Sherman, who remained as head coach.

Thompson and Sherman enjoyed a respectful relationship, but the two men were not friends, and it didn't help that Sherman still believed that he was the right man to be the GM.

The 2005 season was a disaster for the Packers, who lost their first four games and never recovered. Favre tried to do too much with a limited talent base and threw a staggering 29 interceptions as Green Bay finished 4–12, the team's worst record since 1991.

On January 2, 2006, in a move that surprised some fans and certainly many Packers players, Thompson fired Sherman, despite the fact that the coach had posted a career record of 53–27 and led the team to three division titles.

Now this really *was* Thompson's team.

Into the Storm

Ted Thompson faced two major issues at the conclusion of the Packers' miserable 2005 campaign. The first involved the direction in which he planned to go after firing head coach Mike Sherman. Second, he had to deal with Brett Favre, who, after the season, spoke seriously about retiring. Thompson knew that whomever he hired as the new head coach had to connect with and inspire his veteran quarterback.

Mike McCarthy was named the Packers' new head coach in 2006, replacing Mike Sherman.

Thompson interviewed, among others, Dallas Cowboys offensive coordinator Sean Payton, San Diego Chargers defensive coordinator Wade Phillips, New York Giants offensive coordinator Maurice Carthon, and Packers defensive coordinator Jim Bates; the name of former Packers quarterbacks coach—and Brett Favre confidant—Steve Mariucci was also mentioned. Even Favre's agent, James "Bus" Cook, suggested that if Mariucci was hired, Favre would almost certainly be back for the 2006 season.

So it came as a bit of a shock on January 12, 2006, when Thompson, with the backing of the executive committee, selected a new head coach—Mike McCarthy, who had just finished his first season as the San Francisco 49ers' offensive coordinator.

Though only 42 years old, McCarthy was viewed as a creative offensive mind. Although he'd never served as a head coach before, McCarthy did have coaching experience with the 49ers, Kansas City Chiefs, and New Orleans Saints, and had been the Packers' quarterbacks coach in 1999 under Ray Rhodes, where he developed a good working relationship with Favre.

But Favre was still undecided about his future and spent several months in a strange, strained dance with the team. At one point, word leaked that Favre would announce his decision at his annual golf tournament in Hattiesburg, Mississippi, which prompted a flurry of national media to descend upon the charity event to hear what he had to say.

As it turned out, he said nothing. Claiming it was simply a rumor and that he had no intention of making an announcement, Favre told the media that they'd wasted their time.

Eventually, Favre realized that his indecision was growing tiresome, so just before training camp, he decided to play at least one more season with what had become the youngest team in the NFL.

McCarthy used Favre brilliantly during the 2006 season. He asked his quarterback to make smart, quick decisions in an attempt to cut down on his interceptions. In return, he put Favre in positions where he could have fun again.

Brett Favre looks for a receiver during a 2006 game. After a disastrous 4–12 season in 2005, the Pack went 8–8 in 2006.

That season, Favre threw a career-high 613 passes for 3,885 yards with 18 touchdown passes and 18 interceptions. More importantly, behind McCarthy and Favre, the Packers had a surprisingly solid 8–8 season, which included a season-ending four-game winning streak.

The future looked bright again.

All Packers, All the Time

The Green Bay Packers are big in Wisconsin. That's not news. Indeed, there are 47 radio affiliates that carry Packers games throughout the state, covering every mile from Hayward in the north to Janesville in the south, from Sheboygan in the east to LaCrosse in the west.

But the Packers are so big that coverage has burst across state borders. There are five radio affiliates in Michigan's Upper Peninsula, which has long been a Packers hotbed despite its address. There are also radio affiliates in Bismarck, North Dakota; Sioux Falls, South Dakota; Des Moines, Iowa; and even in Stillwater, Minnesota—deep in the heart of Vikings country.

Packers fans are perhaps the most loyal in the NFL. Attend a Packers road game anywhere—especially in a warm-weather location—and witness for yourself how many fans are rooting for Green Bay. Packer Backers plan vacations to Miami or Tampa or San Diego to watch their team—especially if it means getting out of the deep freeze of Wisconsin late in a season.

Faithful Packer Backers can be found anywhere, even in Tampa during this September 28, 2008, game against the Buccaneers.

Then there are the "snowbirds" who spend their summers in Wisconsin and head south to the warmth in the winter. They too get tickets to watch their team at rival stadiums.

This phenomenon has existed for years, but it was especially prominent in the mid- to late 1990s, when the Packers were in the midst of their most recent heyday. In 1997, for example, Buccaneers quarterback Trent Dilfer complained bitterly that the crowd in attendance at a December game at Tampa Stadium was predominantly rooting for the Packers. It led the Bucs to change their policy for ticket distribution to ensure that most of the tickets went to home-team fans.

For those who can't go in person, there is the Packers' radio network, which features play-by-play from Wayne Larrivee and color commentary from former Packers star Larry McCarren. Then there's Packers.com, which allows fans to follow games on the Internet. Daily audio clips, video clips, transcripts of press conferences, and podcasts keep fans updated on everything that's happening in the world of the Packers. And don't forget the site's live web cams of Lambeau Field.

Some fans even choose to watch the game on TV with the sound muted while listening to the radio broadcast with Larrivee and McCarren and following the stats online at Packers.com.

Packers fans just can't get enough of a good thing.

Former Packers star Larry McCarren (left) and veteran sportscaster Wayne Larrivee have been calling Packers games together since 1999.

Sweet Charity

The Green Bay Packers have always keenly understood their place in the community and, for years, have done their part to give back to the people who have meant so much to them.

Many players have their own individual charities to which they have pledged time and money, including wide receiver Donald Driver, whose foundation benefits the homeless. And when Brett Favre left the Packers before the 2008 season, Driver took up hosting his annual charity softball game. The first post-Favre iteration of the game drew nearly 6,000 fans to nearby Appleton, Wisconsin, in June 2008.

As an organization, the Packers have three main charitable outlets—the Bishop's Charities Game, the Upper Midwest Shrine Game, and the Green Bay Packers Foundation. The Bishop's Charities Game, usually the first home preseason game,

Since 1950, the Packers have donated a portion of the ticket sales from a preseason game to the Shriners' Hospitals.

was started in 1961. Each year, the team donates a set amount that has added up to more than $3.4 million for the Catholic Diocese of Green Bay.

The Upper Midwest Shrine Game was started in 1950 and is almost always the Packers' final home preseason game. The Packers donate a percentage of the ticket sales to—and have raised more than $3.1 million for—the Shriners' Hospitals for Children.

The Green Bay Packers Foundation, which was formed in 1986 by then-team president Robert Parins, donates money to organizations in need throughout the community and the state.

From the hundreds of requests it receives each year, the team decides which charities it will support based on immediate need.

Need a Ride?

A tradition that began in the Vince Lombardi era has become one of the most endearing and enduring examples of community involvement in football. During training camp, children offer their bikes to Packers players to ride from the locker room to the practice field and back again. Along the way, each kid usually gets to carry the player's helmet and ride on the back of the bike or run alongside it. When the trip is over, the player often gives the bike's owner a pair of sweatbands or some other token of thanks.

At the height of training camp, most players take advantage of the bike swap. Indeed, there are now tips on the Packers' Web site for kids who want to have their bikes used. "Remember," the guidelines say, "if you're a young Packers fan and you want a player to ride your bike, be courteous—it will help your chances."

It's a long-standing Packers tradition that players borrow bicycles from young fans and pedal them to and from practice during training camp.

In 2008, the team donated nearly $160,000 to more than 20 nonprofit organizations. Since the start of the Green Bay Packers Foundation, the team has donated more than $1.8 million to charity.

Since 1961, each year that the Packers have won a world title, they've also won the Bishop's Charities Game.

Cold Reality

There are seasons that come out of nowhere—completely unexpected—and seem to defy all logical explanations. Such was the case with the 2007 Packers. They were expected to be better after an '06 campaign that saw Green Bay—the youngest team in the league, with an average age of 24—improve to 8–8. But in 2007, the Packers exceeded all expectations yet, in the curious milieu that is pro sports, ended up with what proved to be a disappointing season in the final analysis.

These Packers played with the kind of youthful abandon characteristic of a team that initially believed that little was expected of it. And leading the way was the 38-year-old Favre, who was playing with guys who'd had posters of him hanging on their walls when they were kids.

Nevertheless, Favre continued to set records in 2007. He broke one of the NFL's most respected marks on September 30 against the Vikings, when he connected for his 421st career touchdown pass, which broke Dan Marino's record. In that same game, he also broke Marino's record for most career passing attempts (8,358). Another of Marino's records fell on December 16 against the St. Louis Rams when Favre completed a seven-yard pass to Donald Driver to establish a new career passing yards record with 61,362.

Brett Favre fires his record-setting 421st career touchdown toss on September 30, 2007, against the Vikings at the Metrodome.

As the wins piled up, many Packers fans, as well as NFL observers, began to think that the Packers might be the season's "team of destiny." Green Bay finished 13–3, suffering two losses to the Bears and one to the Cowboys in which Favre had to leave in the second quarter with an injury.

The Packers soared into the postseason. After falling behind Seattle 14–0 early in the first quarter of their divisional playoff game, the Pack woke up and buried the Seahawks 42–20 in the snow of Green Bay. That set up the NFC championship game on January 20, 2008, at Lambeau Field. The Packers faced off against the New York Giants, who had won two straight road games to get to this stage.

With windchills that cracked the –25 degree mark (making it the third-coldest playoff game in NFL history), the Packers saw their best chance at returning to the Super Bowl disappear before 2007's real team of destiny.

Though they were outplayed all night, the Packers did manage to force the game into overtime before Favre was intercepted by Corey Webster. Just three plays later, Lawrence Tynes kicked a 47-yard field goal to give the Giants a 23–20 win. A season that had started with few expectations ended with crushing disappointment for Packers fans, who saw this as their best and last chance to see Favre back in the Super Bowl.

They had no idea then how right they were.

Ryan Grant (25) trudges through the snow to score a touchdown as the Packers blew past the Seahawks 42–20 in a divisional playoff game on January 12, 2008.

An End and a Beginning

It should've been simple—painful, perhaps, but inevitable. When the news struck like a thunderbolt on March 4, 2008, that, after 17 seasons, Brett Favre was retiring from the Packers and from football, it should have been a time to reflect on a remarkable career by a remarkable player.

The torch had been passed from Favre—who had started an NFL record 253 straight games dating back to September 27, 1992—to third-year man Aaron Rodgers.

And while that should have been the end of it, anyone who knew Favre knew nothing was that easy. As soon as he announced his retirement, there were those who speculated that he would not be able to stay away from the game. And over the next three years, he continued to dominate the NFL landscape in ways he probably didn't even anticipate.

It began with Favre's decision to change his mind in the summer of 2008. He wanted to return to the Packers but, in point of fact, the Packers had moved on to the 2005 first-round draft pick Rodgers who had shown so much potential.

In a disastrous public relations move that worked for no one, the Packers ultimately ended up trading Favre to the New York Jets. Green Bay received a third-round pick in the 2009 draft for the future Hall of Famer.

His one season with the Jets was plagued by a late-season arm injury. After that season, Favre again contemplated retirement and was released by New York. Now a free agent, Favre finally got what he wanted all along, a chance to play with the Minnesota Vikings, a team on the verge of being a true Super Bowl contender—not to mention a team in the same division as the Packers.

He took advantage of it, too. Playing like a kid again, the 40-year-old Favre had what in many ways was the finest season of his career. He threw for 4,202 yards (his best total since 1998) and 33 touchdowns (his best since 2003). He led the Vikings to a 12–4 record, beating the Packers twice along the way, and Min-

nesota reached the NFC title game. But a disastrous interception late in the game against the New Orleans Saints ended the dream.

In 2010, Favre again agonized over retiring, but he was persuaded to return when three Vikings teammates flew to his Mississippi compound to convince him. In retrospect, they should have stayed home.

The season was a disaster almost from the outset. Favre was injured numerous times, and the Vikings fell from Super Bowl contender to also-rans. In a final indignity, even his storied consecutive games starting streak ended at 297 when a shoulder injury sidelined him in December.

Meanwhile, the Packers did indeed move on. From the outset of his career, Rodgers earned a spot as one of the top quarterbacks in the league.

It was a sight that no one thought they'd ever see: On August 7, 2008, Brett Favre was introduced as the new quarterback of the New York Jets.

PACKERS PARAPHERNALIA

In December 2007, at age 38, Brett Favre was named one of the best signal-callers in the NFL, but his days in a Packers uniform were numbered.

This remarkably lifelike Brett Favre figurine is a treasured keepsake for any Packers fan.

After 16 seasons with Green Bay, Brett Favre's last day in a Packers uniform came on January 20, 2008, although no one knew it at the time.

Brett Favre signed this contract in 1994, and it remained in effect until February 1999.

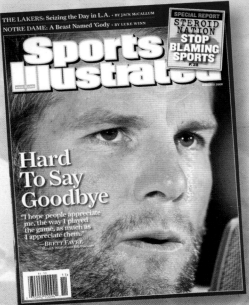

Sports Illustrated

THE LAKERS: Seizing the Day in L.A. - BY JACK McCALLUM
NOTRE DAME: A Beast Named 'Gody - BY LUKE WINN

SPECIAL REPORT
STEROID NATION
STOP BLAMING SPORTS P. 28

Hard
To Say
Goodbye

"I hope people appreciate me, the way I played the game, as much as I appreciate them."
—BRETT FAVRE

When Brett Favre called it quits in March 2008, it made the cover of *Sports Illustrated*. But his retirement was short-lived.

FAVRE
MVP
The Right Choice

ELECT ☑ FAVRE
★ ★ ★ ★ MVP

During the Brett Favre era (1992–2007), every year was an election year in Green Bay, as far as Packers fans were concerned.

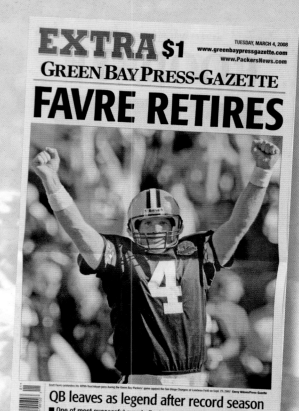

EXTRA $1
TUESDAY, MARCH 4, 2008
www.greenbaypressgazette.com
www.PackersNews.com

GREEN BAY PRESS-GAZETTE
FAVRE RETIRES

QB leaves as legend after record season
■ One of most successful eras in Packers history comes to close / 2
■ Mike Vandermause column: Life will never be the same / 3

The *Press-Gazette* put out a special edition on March 4, 2008, after Brett Favre announced his retirement.

OUR FAVRE

Our Favre
Who art in Lambeau,
Hallowed be thine arm.
The bowl will come
It will be won,
In New Orleans as it is in Lambeau.
Give us this Sunday
Our weekly win,
And give us many touchdown passes
But do not let others pass against us.
Lead us not into frustration
But deliver us to Bourbon Street.
For thine is the MVP, the best of the NFC,
And the glory of the cheeseheads, now and
forever.

Go get 'em!

PACKERS

If Lambeau Field is a shrine, then Brett Favre was the messiah of the Cheeseheads. Clearly, he answered their prayers.

Everything the man touched turned to gold. An autographed Brett Favre helmet, like this one, can fetch as much as $800 on eBay.

NEW YORK POST
METRO EDITION

B'way Brett!

To Packers fans, it was like pouring salt into a wound when Brett Favre was traded to the New York Jets in August 2008.

A Promise Unfulfilled

As the 2008 season dawned, the Packers faced the kind of soaring expectations unseen in Green Bay since the days Mike Holmgren prowled the sidelines and Brett Favre took snaps under center.

The Packers were coming off a 14–4 season in 2007 that ended in overtime in the NFC Championship Game. Nearly every key player (except, of course, Favre) was back and now the team had the kind of experience that was invaluable.

But after a promising 2–0 start, injuries, inconsistency, and especially a poor defense sent the '08 Packers reeling to a 6–10 campaign. At the end of the season, Mike McCarthy took the blame but then turned proactive, firing nearly the entire defensive coaching staff, including coordinator Bob Sanders.

The new defensive coordinator would be wily veteran Dom Capers, who scrapped the Packers' traditional 4–3 defense and went to a more aggressive 3–4.

The results in 2009 were there for all to see. The Packers rode the NFC's best defense and third-best offense to an 11–5 record. Aaron Rodgers, who had played well in his first season as a starter in 2008, was even better in '09, throwing for 4,434 yards and 30 touchdowns.

The Packers returned to the playoffs, facing the Arizona Cardinals in a game few would forget. The Packers fell behind 17–0 in the first quarter

Running back DeShawn Wynn (42) breaks away for a 73-yard TD run in the Packers' 31–21 win over Detroit.

Wondrous Woodson

Charles Woodson has gotten better with age.

When he came to the Packers prior to the 2006 season, after eight mostly disappointing seasons with the Oakland Raiders, Woodson was considered all but finished in the NFL. But he played well his first three seasons as Green Bay's stalwart cornerback, intercepting 19 passes (returning four for touchdowns) and averaging 50 tackles a season. But he improved on that in the 2009 and 2010 seasons.

In 2009, Woodson picked off nine passes, returning three for scores, and he recorded 74 tackles and 18 passes defended on his way to being named NFL Defensive Player of the Year.

In some ways, he was even better in 2010. Though he intercepted only two passes, both came in key situations, and he had more tackles. He also became, perhaps, the team's most eloquent spokesman. Indeed, it was his emotional speech at halftime of Super Bowl XLV, after he was sidelined by injury, that helped propel the Packers to victory.

Veteran cornerback Charles Woodson, who joined the Pack in 2006, has proven to be a steady and supportive addition.

and trailed 31–10 in the third quarter when Rodgers caught fire. He led Green Bay on five straight scoring drives, finally tying the game at 45–45 in the final two minutes and forcing overtime.

But in flash, it was over. On the first drive of OT, Rodgers was hit and fumbled, and Arizona's Karlos Dansby returned the loose ball for the touchdown and incredible 51–45 win. It was a loss that would stay with Rodgers, and the Packers, for months.

Passing the Test

When Aaron Rodgers ran out on the field in the Packers' 2008 preseason opener against the Cincinnati Bengals, Lambeau Field erupted in cheers. And under his facemask you could see Rodgers smile, take a deep breath, and then go about the job he was hired to do.

It had been no picnic for the Packers former first-round pick in the 2005 draft. He sat for three years behind the indestructible Brett Favre waiting for the chance to prove what he could do. And when Rodgers finally got that opportunity, there was no stopping him.

In his first two seasons as the Packers' starter, Rodgers threw for 4,038 yards and 4,434 yards, the first NFL quarterback to ever have consecutive 4,000-yard passing seasons in his first two years as a starter. He also connected for 58 touchdown passes with just 20 interceptions. But if there were knocks on Rodgers those first two years, they were his seeming inability to direct late-game rallies and, worse, failure in the postseason.

But in 2010, all the fears faded, and he became the new face of the Green Bay Packers, replacing—perhaps once and for all—the sour memories of Favre's departure.

Rodgers directed a number of late-game rallies on the way to Green Bay's 10–6 season, throwing for 3,922 yards and 28 touchdowns despite missing one game with a concussion.

But it was late in the season and in the playoffs when he truly flourished. Knowing the Packers had to win their last two regular season games just to make it into the postseason, Rodgers orchestrated wins over the New York Giants and Chicago Bears.

Once in the postseason, he led the Packers to three straight road playoff victories over the Philadelphia Eagles, Atlanta Falcons, and Bears. In those three games, he threw for a total of 790 yards and six touchdowns and ran for two more. The highlight was the second-round triumph over the top-seeded Falcons when Rodgers was 31 of 36 for 366 yards and three touchdowns in a performance many veteran NFL observers called a "perfect" game.

Then, of course, came Super Bowl XLV, when Rodgers shook off any nerves, threw for 304 yards and three touchdowns, and was named the game's MVP.

"We put the game on his shoulders and he took it from there," coach Mike McCarthy said simply.

Aaron Rodgers (12) stood patiently in Brett Favre's shadow for three seasons before finally taking his spot under center.

In 2008, in his first season as the Packers' starting quarterback, Aaron Rodgers threw for more than 4,000 yards, but Green Bay struggled to a 6–10 record.

Packers a Hit at XLV

In its long and storied history, the Green Bay Packers franchise never experienced a season like 2010. Who could've made up such a thing?

Considered a Super Bowl contender in the preseason thanks to a young, talented cast, Green Bay seemed prepared to at least make a run for the franchise's 13th world title, its fourth Super Bowl title, and its first Lombardi Trophy since the 1996 season.

But it would be a long journey from beginning to end, fraught with uncertainties, inconsistencies, and injuries to key personnel

Packer safety Nick Collins dives for the end zone after returning an interception 37 yards in Super Bowl XLV. Journeyman defensive lineman Howard Green hit Ben Roethlisberger to force the errant pass in the first quarter.

sustained at what seemed to be almost biblical proportions. In the end, though, all that tribulation helped rocket the Packers into Super Bowl XLV and an eventual, grueling 31–25 victory over the Pittsburgh Steelers at Cowboys Stadium.

"This is what it's all about," said coach Mike McCarthy, a Pittsburgh native who had come under his share of withering criticism from Packers fans who felt he was a great coach on Monday through Saturday but lacked a certain something when the game began.

"We're bringing the Vince Lombardi back home to Titletown," said quarterback Aaron Rodgers, who, in his third year after replacing Brett Favre as the starter, had made the team his own by virtue of stellar, almost perfect, play during a six-game win streak. "This is incredible."

Most of the season was, indeed, incredible, but not for the reasons Rodgers espoused. This was a Packers team that suffered through arguably the worst spate of injuries in the NFL. That list was long and varied, including the loss for the season of a number of key starters. Running back Ryan Grant, linebackers Nick Barnett and Brandon Chillar, promising rookie safety Morgan Burnett, and defensive tackle Justin Harrell were at the top of that list. Perhaps most devastating of all, tight end Jermichael Finley, who was developing into a legitimate NFL star, was injured in October. In all, the Packers would end up placing 16 players on the injured reserve list, meaning they could not play the rest of the season. And while many teams might have crumbled under such a weight, the Packers merely shrugged it off, went to the next guy and kept playing.

The Packers roller-coaster ride began almost from the start of the season, when they jumped out to a lead over the Philadelphia Eagles, knocked out starting quarterback Kevin Kolb, and then spent the rest of the game chasing backup Michael Vick all over the field before emerging victorious. Later, traveling to Chicago with a 2–0 record, the Pack committed a staggering 18 penalties

What followed was a streak for the ages. The Packers, needing to win their last two regular-season games to reach the playoffs, did just that—crushing the New York Giants and beating the Bears. Slipping in the postseason as the sixth, and last, seed in the NFC, the Packers went on the road to beat the Eagles and the Atlanta Falcons. In the NFC title game, the Packers knocked off the hated Bears to improbably reach the Super Bowl.

Jordy Nelson (87) dives for the end zone in Super Bowl XLV, past Troy Polamalu. Nelson came up three yards short. Emerging as Green Bay's go-to receiver, he snagged nine catches for 140 yards and one TD.

Once there, the Packers put their hopes and dreams on Rodgers's right arm, and he delivered. He threw three touchdown passes, including a decisive fourth-quarter TD to Greg Jennings. The defense, despite another tough injury to cornerback Charles Woodson, held on for the 31–25 win.

Rodgers threw for 304 yards and was named the MVP, the Packers first Super Bowl MVP quarterback since Bart Starr.

Greg Jennings stands triumphant after catching a fourth-quarter 8-yard TD pass from Aaron Rodgers in Super Bowl XLV. The score increased the Packers' lead to 28–17 at that point and proved to be the winning touchdown.

in a three-point loss to the Bears. From that strange beginning, it only got more interesting.

Green Bay played superbly at times, shutting out the New York Jets and routing the Dallas Cowboys, for example. But the Packers could be just as horrible, losing games to the Washington Redskins and the Miami Dolphins, and suffering what appeared to be a crushing defeat to the Detroit Lions.

The Packers faced an almost must-win in December on the road against the powerful Patriots without Rodgers (who was sidelined with a concussion). Backup QB Matt Flynn played superbly, and the defense slowed down league MVP quarterback Tom Brady. A late Packers' rally was snuffed out, however, and the team fell to New England 31–27, giving Green Bay an 8–6 record. But in defeat, the Packers found something special.

"Even with the loss, we knew we were a good team," Rodgers said. "So we said to ourselves, 'Let's not lose this opportunity.'"

PACKERS PARAPHERNALIA

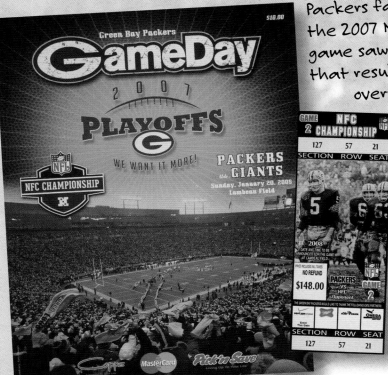

Packers fans who attended the 2007 NFC championship game saw a tight match that resulted in a 23–20 overtime loss to the Giants. Little did they know that they had also witnessed Brett Favre's last game as a Packer.

This program (top) is from Super Bowl XLV. Green Bay Mayor Jim Schmitt used these tickets (above left) after having made a friendly wager with Luke Ravenstahl, the mayor of Pittsburgh. As the loser of the bet, Mayor Ravenstahl agreed to shovel snow off the walkways of St. Rosalia—the church of Pittsburgh-born Packers coach Mike McCarthy's parents.

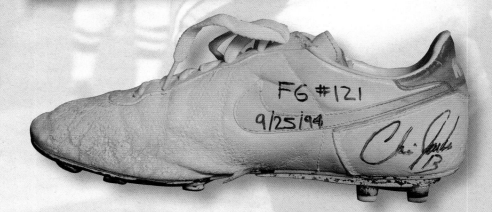

On September 25, 1994, kicker Chris Jacke set a new Packers record for field goals made. That day, he surpassed Chester Marcol's mark of 120. Jacke's 173 career field goals now rank second behind Ryan Longwell (226).

No doubt about it, Packer Backers are the most loyal fans in the NFL.

The Packers were once again the NFL's "Big Cheese" (above right) according to the *Milwaukee Journal Sentinel*, which also noted that Green Bay reclaimed its moniker of "Titletown" (above).

This cap celebrates Super Bowl XLV, which featured two of the NFL's most storied franchises, the Packers and the Pittsburgh Steelers.

PACKERS SEASON RECORDS

1919–Today

Year	Head Coach	Record	Result	Postseason/Notes
1919	Curly Lambeau	10–1	n/a	—
1920	Curly Lambeau	9–1–1	n/a	—

Packers join the American Professional Football Association (APFA)

Year	Head Coach	Record	Result	Postseason/Notes
1921	Curly Lambeau	3–2–1	7th	—

APFA becomes the National Football League (NFL)

Year	Head Coach	Record	Result	Postseason/Notes
1922	Curly Lambeau	4–3–3	8th	—
1923	Curly Lambeau	7–2–1	3rd	—
1924	Curly Lambeau	7–4	6th	—
1925	Curly Lambeau	8–5	9th	—
1926	Curly Lambeau	7–3–3	5th	—
1927	Curly Lambeau	7–2–1	2nd	—
1928	Curly Lambeau	6–4–3	4th	—
1929	Curly Lambeau	12–0–1	1st	Title #1
1930	Curly Lambeau	10–3–1	1st	Title #2
1931	Curly Lambeau	12–2	1st	Title #3
1932	Curly Lambeau	10–3–1	2nd	—

NFL Realignment: Packers join NFL Western Division

Year	Head Coach	Record	Result	Postseason/Notes
1933	Curly Lambeau	5–7–1	3rd	—
1934	Curly Lambeau	7–6	3rd	—
1935	Curly Lambeau	8–4	2nd	—
1936	Curly Lambeau	10–1–1	1st	NFL: beat Boston Redskins 21–6 Title #4
1937	Curly Lambeau	7–4	2nd	—
1938	Curly Lambeau	8–3	1st	NFL: lost to New York Giants 23–17
1939	Curly Lambeau	9–2	1st	NFL: beat New York Giants 27–0 Title #5
1940	Curly Lambeau	6–4–1	2nd	—
1941	Curly Lambeau	10–1	1st	West: lost to Chicago Bears 33–14
1942	Curly Lambeau	8–2–1	2nd	—
1943	Curly Lambeau	7–2–1	2nd	—

Year	Head Coach	Record	Result	Postseason/Notes
1944	Curly Lambeau	8–2	1st	NFL: beat New York Giants 14–7 Title #6
1945	Curly Lambeau	6–4	3rd	—
1946	Curly Lambeau	6–5	3rd	—
1947	Curly Lambeau	6–5–1	3rd	—
1948	Curly Lambeau	3–9	4th	—
1949	Curly Lambeau	2–10	5th	—

NFL Realignment: Packers join NFL National Conference

Year	Head Coach	Record	Result	Postseason/Notes
1950	Gene Ronzani	3–9	5th	—
1951	Gene Ronzani	3–9	5th	—
1952	Gene Ronzani	6–6	4th	—

NFL Realignment: Packers join NFL Western Conference

Year	Head Coach	Record	Result	Postseason/Notes
1953	Gene Ronzani	2–7–1	—	—
	Devore/McLean	0–2	6th	—
1954	Lisle Blackbourn	4–8	5th	—
1955	Lisle Blackbourn	6–6	3rd	—
1956	Lisle Blackbourn	4–8	5th	—
1957	Lisle Blackbourn	3–9	6th	—
1958	Ray McLean	1–10–1	6th	—
1959	Vince Lombardi	7–5	3rd	—
1960	Vince Lombardi	8–4	1st	NFL: lost to Philadelphia Eagles 17–13
1961	Vince Lombardi	11–3	1st	NFL: beat New York Giants 37–0 Title #7
1962	Vince Lombardi	13–1	1st	NFL: beat New York Giants 16–7 Title #8
1963	Vince Lombardi	11–2–1	2nd	—
1964	Vince Lombardi	8–5–1	2nd	—
1965	Vince Lombardi	10–3–1	1st	NFL: beat Cleveland Browns 23–12 Title #9

Year	Head Coach	Record	Result	Postseason/Notes
1966	Vince Lombardi	12–2	1st	NFL: beat Dallas Cowboys 34–27
				SB: beat Kansas City Chiefs 35–10
				Title #10

NFL Realignment: Packers join NFL Central Division

Year	Head Coach	Record	Result	Postseason/Notes
1967	Vince Lombardi	9–4–1	1st	West: beat Los Angeles Rams 28–7
				NFL: beat Dallas Cowboys 21–17
				SB: beat Oakland Raiders 33–14
				Title #11
1968	Phil Bengtson	6–7–1	3rd	—
1969	Phil Bengtson	8–6	3rd	—

NFL Realignment: Packers join NFC Central

Year	Head Coach	Record	Result	Postseason/Notes
1970	Phil Bengtson	6–8	3rd	—
1971	Dan Devine	4–8–2	4th	—
1972	Dan Devine	10–4	1st	Div: lost to Washington Redskins 16–3
1973	Dan Devine	5–7–2	3rd	—
1974	Dan Devine	6–8	3rd	—
1975	Bart Starr	4–10	3rd	—
1976	Bart Starr	5–9	4th	—
1977	Bart Starr	4–10	4th	—
1978	Bart Starr	8–7–1	2nd	—
1979	Bart Starr	5–11	4th	—
1980	Bart Starr	5–10–1	4th	—
1981	Bart Starr	8–8	2nd	—
1982	Bart Starr	5–3–1	1st*	Round 1: beat St. Louis Cardinals 41–16
				Round 2: lost to Dallas Cowboys 37–26
1983	Bart Starr	8–8	2nd	—
1984	Forrest Gregg	8–8	2nd	—
1985	Forrest Gregg	8–8	2nd	—
1986	Forrest Gregg	4–12	4th	—
1987	Forrest Gregg	5–9–1	3rd	—
1988	Lindy Infante	4–12	5th	—
1989	Lindy Infante	10–6	2nd	—
1990	Lindy Infante	6–10	4th	—
1991	Lindy Infante	4–12	4th	—
1992	Mike Holmgren	9–7	2nd	—
1993	Mike Holmgren	9–7	2nd	WC: beat Detroit Lions 28–24
				Div: lost to Dallas Cowboys 27–17

Year	Head Coach	Record	Result	Postseason/Notes
1994	Mike Holmgren	9–7	2nd	WC: beat Detroit Lions 16–12
				Div: lost to Dallas Cowboys 35–9
1995	Mike Holmgren	11–5	1st	WC: beat Atlanta Falcons 37–20
				Div: beat San Francisco 49ers 27–17
				NFC: lost to Dallas Cowboys 38–27
1996	Mike Holmgren	13–3	1st	Div: beat San Francisco 49ers 35–14
				NFC: beat Carolina Panthers 30–13
				SB: beat New England Patriots 35–21
				Title #12
1997	Mike Holmgren	13–3	1st	Div: beat Tampa Bay Buccaneers 21–7
				NFC: beat San Francisco 49ers 23–10
				SB: lost to Denver Broncos 31–24
1998	Mike Holmgren	11–5	2nd	WC: lost to San Francisco 49ers 30–27
1999	Ray Rhodes	8–8	4th	—
2000	Mike Sherman	9–7	3rd	—
2001	Mike Sherman	12–4	2nd	WC: beat San Francisco 49ers 25–15
				Div: lost to St. Louis Rams 45–17

NFL Realignment: Packers join NFC North

Year	Head Coach	Record	Result	Postseason/Notes
2002	Mike Sherman	12–4	1st	WC: lost to Atlanta Falcons 27–7
2003	Mike Sherman	10–6	1st	WC: beat Seattle Seahawks 33–27
				Div: lost to Philadelphia Eagles 20–17
2004	Mike Sherman	10–6	1st	WC: lost to Minnesota Vikings 31–17
2005	Mike Sherman	4–12	4th	—
2006	Mike McCarthy	8–8	2nd	—
2007	Mike McCarthy	13–3	1st	Div: beat Seattle Seahawks 42–20
				NFC: lost to New York Giants 23–20
2008	Mike McCarthy	6–10	3rd	—
2009	Mike McCarthy	11–5	2nd	WC: lost to Arizona Cardinals 51–45
2010	Mike McCarthy	10–6	2nd	WC: beat Philadelphia Eagles 21–16
				Div: beat Atlanta Falcons 48–21
				NFC: beat Chicago Bears 21–14
				SB: beat Pittsburgh Steelers 31–25
				Title #13

* Strike-shortened season. Playoffs were expanded and teams were seeded according to over-all record rather than divisional standing. Packers were seeded third in the NFC.

NFL—NFL championship game; West—Western Division/Conference championship game; SB—Super Bowl; Div—Divisional round game; WC—Wild Card round game; NFC—NFC championship game

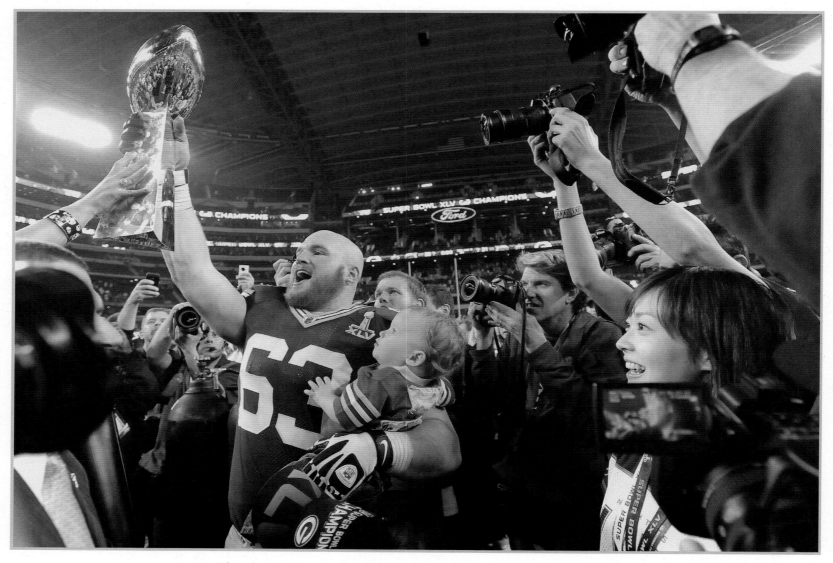

The whole Packers family shares in the celebration after Super Bowl XLV,
as center Scott Wells hoists the Vince Lombardi Trophy while son Kingston looks on.

INDEX

GENUINE
Draft
JOHN DEERE
10 Yds to Go
4 Ball On
4 Quarter
11:32
RETIRED NUMBERS
14
DON HUTSON
3
TONY CANADEO
END ZONE
76
25
FAVRE
4
63